TO BARCELONA AND BACK

ALSO BY PAMELA SARGENT

Novels

Cloned Lives
The Sudden Star
The Golden Space
The Alien Upstairs
The Shore of Women
Alien Child
Ruler of the Sky: A Novel of Genghis Khan
Climb the Wind: A Novel of Another America
Season of the Cats

The Watchstar Trilogy

Watchstar
Eye of the Comet
Homesmind

The Venus Trilogy

Venus of Dreams
Venus of Shadows
Child of Venus

The Seed Trilogy

Earthseed
Farseed
Seed Seeker

Short Fiction

Starshadows
The Best of Pamela Sargent
Behind the Eyes of Dreamers and Other Short Novels
The Mountain Cage and Other Stories
Dream of Venus and Other Stories
Puss in D.C. and Other Stories
Eye of Flame and Other Fantasies
Thumbprints

Nonfiction

Firebrands: The Heroines of Science Fiction and Fantasy (with Ron Miller)

Anthologies

Women of Wonder
Bio-Futures
More Women of Wonder
The New Women of Wonder
Afterlives (with Ian Watson)
Women of Wonder, The Classic Years
Women of Wonder, The Contemporary Years
Nebula Awards 29
Nebula Awards 30
Nebula Awards 31
Conqueror Fantastic

Star Trek Novels (with George Zebrowski)

A Fury Scorned (The Next Generation)
Heart of the Sun (The Original Series)
Across the Universe (The Original Series)
Garth of Izar (The Original Series)

TO BARCELONA AND BACK

ONE WRITER'S TOUR OF SPAIN

PAMELA SARGENT

WILDSIDE PRESS

Copyright © 2024 by Pamela Sargent
Published by Wildside Press LLC.
wildsidepress.com

INTRODUCTION

Sometime in late 1993, my editor at Crown Publishers informed me that Edhasa, the Spanish publisher of my historical novel *Ruler of the Sky*, a novel about Genghis Khan that came out at the beginning of that year, wanted to bring me to Spain for a publicity tour to promote the book. This came as a shock, especially given that the state of my writing career at the time was extremely precarious.

In late 1992, Bantam, the publisher of my first two novels about a terraformed Venus, *Venus of Dreams* and *Venus of Shadows*, abruptly cancelled the contract for the third novel of the trilogy, which I was in the middle of completing. The excuse given to me was that I had been taking too long with the third book, missing my deadline by ages, although the real reason seemed to be that the publisher was cancelling contracts largely to save money while taking the opportunity to get rid of writers who were deemed unprofitable or disagreeable. My trilogy, it seemed, was destined to remain incomplete and eventually die.

In addition to this blow, I had lost Lisa Healy, the editor who had bought *Ruler of the Sky* for Crown (she was also the editor for my science fiction novel *The Shore of Women* and we had worked well together), when she left Crown for a job at another publisher. But not to worry, Lisa told me, as an editor handpicked by her with some power within the company would be taking over the editing of my novel and was equally enthusiastic about its prospects. A couple of months after that, Lisa's choice for my editor also left Crown for another job and I was left with an editor who had little interest in promoting my book or even having much to do with it. There's nothing for an editor who inherits another editor's book to gain from promoting it within the company. *Ruler of the Sky* had become an orphan, as we say in the trade, an apt description since such books are basically left to fend for themselves in the marketplace with smaller printings and little publicity. The editor who worked with me most closely on *Ruler of the Sky* was Alison Samuel, my British editor at Chatto &

Windus, and I count her as one of the best editors I have ever had, but by the time the invitation from my Spanish publisher reached me, *Ruler of the Sky* had failed to find any paperback publisher in the U.S.

The unpredictable writing profession is filled with ups and downs. Some of them arrive sequentially and others simultaneously. The news of the cancelled contract from Bantam hit me just before I won a Nebula Award, and the invitation from Spain arrived when I thought *Ruler of the Sky* would be a publishing disaster, with mixed reviews and no paperback sale. I quickly accepted Edhasa's invitation; at the very least, I would have an opportunity to visit Spain and escape my current troubles temporarily.

That trip turned out to be one of the happiest highlights of my life.

By the time I arrived home from my publicity tour of Spain, I was so let down by my return to my troubles that I escaped again by putting together a journal of my trip while it was all still fresh in my mind. I relived the trip in my journal. This book is that journal, originally written only for members of my family (travel for me is largely absorbing my experiences and writing things down as opposed to taking photos), edited and fine-tuned but essentially the same narrative I set down in 1994.

Anyone reading this book will note how different travel was thirty years ago, before the Instagram and selfies-in-front-of-popular-sites era, and no smart phones either. My arrangements for traveling to Spain were largely conducted through faxes and phone calls. Sites that I visited with no problem require reservations now to see them, often in advance of embarking on the trip. Much as I long to return to Barcelona and hope to do so in the not too distant future, the Barcelona I would see now isn't the Barcelona I inhabited for far too brief a time.

Somehow I managed to go on with my writing, however hopeless it seemed at the time, by writing short stories and eventually finding a home for a new novel as well as the third Venus book, *Child of Venus*, with John Douglas at HarperPrism. And in 2019, the Spanish publisher Ediciones Pàmies brought out a new paperback edition of *Ruler of the Sky*.

Sometimes I imagine that my Spanish tour of thirty years ago might have had even more of an effect on me than I realized at the time. My writing had been treated as something worth serious attention, and I could remember that and reflect on it when times were tough. To this day, I remain grateful to all of the people who made my time in Spain so memorable.

Pamela Sargent
Albany, New York
June 23, 2024

TO BARCELONA AND BACK

MONDAY, MAY 2, 1994

The thought came to me sometime near the end of the flight to Barcelona. Pablo Somarriba, my editor at Edhasa, publisher of the Spanish edition of my historical novel *Ruler of the Sky*, was to meet my partner and fellow writer George Zebrowski and me at the airport, and during all the months of writing and faxing to him and to the people at the Institute of North American Studies in Barcelona, I hadn't told anyone what we looked like. How would he recognize us?

"Don't worry," George told me. "He'll probably be holding up a sign with your name on it." Of course I should have thought of that myself.

The first leg of the trip had not gone well. To get from our home in Binghamton, New York to JFK International Airport required taking a Trans-World Express commuter flight to hook up with TWA at JFK. Only TWA and Iberia had direct flights to Barcelona from New York, and only TWA had flights out of Binghamton, which is how we ended up on a propeller-driven plane that seated forty people. The weather was windy, and the plane had to make a stop at Ithaca before heading on to New York. By the time we were heading toward JFK, there was so much turbulence that I was clutching my barf bag tightly and wondering when I was going to start vomiting.

"Just look out the window," George said, "and focus on something in the distance." Doing so didn't help much. By the time we were near JFK, the flight attendant had told us to dump our beverage cups and garbage wherever we could. "If I come to collect it," she announced, "I'll be bouncing off the walls." Soon the pilot was apologizing for the bumpiness of the flight, which didn't boost my confidence. We're all going to die, I thought, torn between terror and nausea. The only passengers enjoying the trip were two eleven-year-old boys across the aisle who kept shouting "Yes! Yes!" every time the plane dipped and shook. When we finally landed, the flight attendant told us that it was the worse flight she'd ever experienced in ten years of flying.

This didn't bode well for the rest of the trip. We stumbled into the TWA terminal on shaky legs and sat down. I was already overwrought, having spent the last two days finishing work on my third speech while packing. The sight of the plane that would carry us across the Atlantic didn't bode well, either; it was a Lockheed 1101 that looked as though it had flown the Atlantic too many times already.

I estimated that at least half the passengers aboard our flight were Spanish. A young Spanish woman seated next to us exchanged a few pleasantries with us, then leaned forward, crossed herself, and began to pray. (I was later to discover that many Spaniards cross themselves and pray on planes, although apparently not on trains, buses, cars, or other forms of transportation.) Another ambiguous omen, I thought.

But the flight went well, even if the food did turn out to be the usual airline toy food and there was no champagne among the free bottles of wine. One of the flight attendants turned out to be a card, cracking jokes whenever she came down the aisle. "You're so cheerful," George said to her at one point, "and the other attendants seem depressed or upset." A conspiratorial look crossed her face. "It's the drugs," she said in a low voice.

There was, I had learned from my travel agent, no such thing as a truly "direct" flight to Barcelona. Any plane going to Barcelona had to stop in Madrid, at which point the Madrid-bound passengers got off and the rest had to battle their jet lag for two hours while security people came aboard, opened the overhead storage compartments, and asked you to identify your baggage. The security people finished their job in about half an hour; the plane sat there on the tarmac while most of us stretched out across empty seats and tried to sleep.

TUESDAY, MAY 3, 1994

It was the morning of Tuesday, May 3rd, by the time we had landed in Madrid. We were supposed to land in Barcelona at around 9:45 AM. Stretched out on a row of seats, trying to sleep and waiting for the airplane to haul ass and head for Barcelona, I was worrying again about the whole trip. What if I made a complete fool of myself? Pablo Somarriba, in his last fax, had seemed extremely agitated, as if expecting things to go wrong. Was he simply a perfectionist, a high-strung man with an excitable temperament, or did he have good reason to think everything was going to be a "disaster," one of the less soothing words he had used in his latest fax? I had composed an extremely reassuring, confident letter and faxed it back to him, but wasn't sure it would do any good.

The plane finally took off, and I managed to repair my makeup and crank up my hair before we landed in Barcelona. The airport turned out to be a huge glassy structure that was a model of efficiency. My guess is that it took us no more than half an hour, and possibly not even that long, to leave the plane, collect our check-through luggage, go through customs and a passport check point, and make our way to the area where Pablo Somarriba was to meet us.

George spotted him first. We couldn't miss him. In his hands, held aloft, was a copy of the Spanish edition of *Ruler of the Sky*. The words GENGIS KAN were emblazoned on the dust jacket in big letters, along with my name, on a gold background. *El soberano del cielo* was the subtitle—"ruler of the sky" in Spanish.

Pablo Somarriba turned out to be a slender, dark-haired, brown-skinned man of about forty, with a mustache and extremely white teeth. He quickly apologized about the copy of my book he had with him; he had brought me one with unbound sheets because the press was still binding the first copies. I didn't mind at all; the book, even in its unbound state, looked wonderful.

We went outside, and Pablo led us to a cab. All the taxis were lined up in an orderly row; we got into the one at the head of the line. (Later on during the trip, I learned more about the practices of cabdrivers in Spain. At airports, taxi stands, and other such places, the drivers line up in order; the passenger is expected to take the cab at the head of the line. No one tries to cut off another driver or steal his business; in fact, if you move toward a cab that isn't at the head of the line, one of the drivers will quickly direct you to the first cab. Often, if there are a lot of cabs, one or two of the drivers at the end of the line will come up to help make sure passengers take cabs in the proper order. This is an entirely voluntary system, enforced by the drivers themselves.)

The airport lies on the outskirts of Barcelona, and there was a fair amount of traffic on the way in. Rush hours, in Spain, can run until ten in the morning and well past seven at night; in Madrid, the rush hour sometimes lasts until close to noon. By now, we were at ease with Pablo, who pointed out various sights along the way. The Plaça Catalunya, a huge open square that is one of the city's central points, with numerous bus and subway stops, was within sight of the hotel where we were headed. Pablo apologized for the Plaça Catalunya, which he considered unattractive, but I found myself liking this plaza; people were sitting, or sometimes lying, around on the grassy spots, and half the city seemed to be out walking on the sidewalks surrounding it. Our hotel, Pablo told us, was centrally located, near the old city (known as the Barri Gòtic) and right on La Rambla. La Rambla, the most famous street in Barcelona! And, as we found out, a place where a party seems to be going on almost twenty-four hours a day.

Pablo helped us check into Le Meridien, our five-star hotel, and a place where we were to discover that the difference between a five-star hotel and a four-star hotel is nearly as wide as the gap that yawns between a four-star hotel and a fleabag. The staff was solicitous from the start; God forbid we should even have to lift our luggage from the trunk of the cab. The jet lag was taking hold by then; I wanted to sleep more than anything else, and knew that was exactly what I couldn't allow myself to do.

Pablo, sounding very apologetic, said that he would have to get back to his office for the rest of the day. Did we need anything? Was there anything he could do? He was at our service if there was anywhere we wanted to go later. I told him that we would probably take an exploratory walk later and turn in early; my scheduled interviews with reporters were to start the next morning at nine, and I wanted to be in good shape for them.

"If there's anything I can do," Pablo said, handing me his business card, "just call. I've written in my home number, too. Call any time if you need anything or have a problem."

I glanced at the card after Pablo had left. It said:

PABLO SOMARRIBA RUEDA
Director Literario y de Promoción
Edhasa

In all the months of faxes and letters, this was the first inkling I had of his actual position. My God, I thought, he isn't just an editor; he's in charge of the whole company.

* * * *

We went up to our room in one of those small European elevators that holds four people at most. We passed a large sitting area, with sofas, chairs, desks, and ashtrays, on our way to the corridor that led to our room.

Our room! I gaped when the porter opened the door. We had a small entryway, a sitting area with a sofa and chairs, a large coffee table, a king-sized bed, and a huge closet and dresser. The bathroom was a Roman sort of job with white tiles and steps leading to the bathtub, while the toilet and bidet were discreetly hidden behind walls. Two large robes of thick white terrycloth hung on the back of the bathroom door, and the hotel also provided white cloth slippers, along with a supply of toilet articles. The whole suite was bigger than our apartment at home, and I soon discovered that we had an outside balcony from which the tall stone spires of Barcelona's Gothic cathedral, one of the city's most famous landmarks, could be seen in the east. In the south, we also had a clear view of Montjuïc, the large hill on which the Olympic stadium was built for the 1992 Summer Olympic Games. An amusement park is also on this hill, and its huge Ferris wheel was clearly visible.

By the time we had unpacked, there was a knock at the door. Another porter entered, carrying a huge floral arrangement of roses and other flowers. The card with the flowers was signed by John Zvereff, Executive Director of the Institute of North American Studies. They had sent me flowers! A little later, another package from the Institute was delivered, an envelope filled with brochures about notable Barcelona sights and a large map of the city.

Pablo had given me a copy of some of the publicity for my book. He had himself translated a short essay I had written about my sources into Spanish, to distribute to booksellers and journalists, and I learned later that he had gone through the translation of my novel line by line, to make sure the translator was both eloquent and accurate; he had even checked up on all the Mongol names, in case their equivalents in Spanish differed. My book, in the new Edhasa catalogue of upcoming releases, was listed next to a novel by Naguib Mahfuz, the Nobel Prize winning Egyptian novelist. This was the kind of publisher that published the work of major literary figures and made me feel my fiction was just as important!

Jet lag and the catalogue's revelations were making me punchy. Maybe I was imagining all this. I went out on the balcony; George had collapsed on the bed by the time I came back inside. "You can't sleep," I warned him. "You can take a nap, but if you go to sleep now, you'll be jetlagged during the entire trip." George moaned and groaned, we both took a short nap, and then compelled ourselves to haul our exhausted bodies downstairs and outside.

It was about three on a sunny afternoon, with the temperature in the seventies. La Rambla is a wide, divided street with a walkway in the middle of two lanes. The newsstands were doing a brisk business, along with several kiosks run by birdsellers; the air was filled with the songs, chirps, and cawings of caged birds.

We wandered for a while. George cut a dashing figure; he had brought his hand-carved wooden Polish cane to use in case his hip acted up, and wore his Panama hat so he wouldn't get sunburned. The newsstands sold not only newspapers, but also postcards, souvenirs, posters, books (paperbacks and hardcovers, everything from Dean Koontz and Stephen King to small volumes by classic writers), and a wide selection of pornography, including stuff for sadomasochists and slews of magazines with nude male models. Some of this was the kind of stuff you'd find in hard-core porn establishments in the U.S., but no one on La Rambla was batting an eye. A few mimes were out, striking poses in their costumes while waiting for people to drop coins in the boxes in front of them. One mime was dressed like a Roman, and covered entirely by metallic paint; he looked like a bronze sculpture. Whenever anyone dropped a coin into his box, he would suddenly change position in a robotic sort of way and then stay in his new pose—for minutes, if necessary—until someone else gave him a coin. There were lots of seats where people could sit down to rest; an old man who looked out for the seats charged only a few pesetas for someone to sit there, and you could sit for as long as you liked. A few blocks down from the hotel, we found one of Barcelona's most popular food markets, full of meats, cheeses, fish, vegetables, and beautifully arranged fresh fruit. It seemed like a good time to stock up on some fruit; George changed some money at an American Express office. Hazily, through the jet lag, I was dimly realizing that eating an early dinner was going to be a problem in a city where none of the restaurants open until eight or nine at the earliest.

We bought a bottle of Cava, the sparkling wine native to the region, and headed back to the hotel. It was nearly six, and we were exhausted. The sensible thing to do was to call room service, eat a light meal in our room, and get to bed early; I had my work cut out for me the next day.

George stored the wine in our room's minibar refrigerator. I was about to sit down on the sofa when I spotted a tall box on the coffee table that had been left there while we were out, opened it, and found a bottle of Rioja, Spain's noted red wine. "Compliments of the Director-General," the card with the box said, meaning the wine was from the hotel manager.

We had the wine with our dinner. It was one of the best wines I've ever had in my life.

WEDNESDAY, MAY 4, 1994

I woke up early, having gone to sleep not long after eight, and felt restored. I lay there for a while, speculating about jet lag and how ridiculous it was that so many people had to suffer and stumble around dementedly during their first day in a European city. It was easy enough to avoid jet lag; all you had to do was take a flight that would land at your destination in the evening, so you could get a good night's sleep and be ready for action the next morning. So naturally most of the airlines schedule trans-Atlantic flights so you land in the morning and have to suffer for hours afterward.

George had slept well, too. The evening before, he had discovered that he could float in our huge bathtub by resting his arms on the tub's armrests and his head on the back of the tub. I made another discovery that morning, a large magnifying mirror near the sink to use while putting on makeup.

We found a note on our doorknob as we left the room. The hotel was apologizing for being unable to provide us with their "customary nighttime service." I supposed that we had gone to bed too early for this nighttime service, whatever it was.

The hotel served breakfast from seven until eleven. A hostess showed us to a table; a glance at the buffet showed me that we weren't just going to get coffee and croissants. They had everything! A huge selection of sliced meats and cheeses for Germans and Scandinavians! Plain croissants, chocolate croissants, and rolls of all kinds for the French and Italians! Jars of granola, bran, and other cereals, next to pitchers of milk, for the health-minded! Bacon and eggs for Americans, and pats of butter for their bread and rolls! Miso soup for the Japanese! Bowls of fresh fruit, stewed fruit, and dried fruit for everybody! We were shown to a table; a waitress poured coffee into our cups. I loaded up at the buffet, remembering that lunch in Spain wasn't eaten until around two-thirty. Every few minutes or so, a waitress came by, whisked away our used plates and silverware, brought us clean ones, and poured more coffee.

Two Americans, a woman and a man, were sitting at my left. I glanced at them sideways, not wanting to stare, and listened. They were apparently there on a business trip, on their way to a conference. The more they talked, the more I disliked them. The woman was putting down acquaintances in a drawling, slightly rusty, finishing-school voice; she didn't have a good word to say about anyone she knew. The man was talking about his ten-year-old daughter, who had called him up long-distance the night before. "What did she want?" the woman asked him. "Oh, I don't know," he replied. "Something with her teeth, or a headache—you know, some childish crisis or other." This guy's a creep, I thought; he's putting down his own daughter in front of a business associate. I looked at them then. The man was an unprepossessing-looking dude with a round face and thinning dark hair; his companion had drab reddish-brown hair in a pageboy, round glasses, and wore a tailored suit. She also had a potbelly, skinny legs, and a plain face that seemed marked by spite. She looked, I thought, like Godzilla.

We finished our breakfast while Godzilla and her associate were still dishing the dirt on their friends and families, then left. I wanted to be in the lobby, ready to go, at a quarter of nine. The weather didn't look good; the sky was gray, threatening rain.

A driver from the Institute of North American Studies was to pick me up and take me to the Institute building, where the interviews would be held. He arrived closer to nine. (I was to discover, as the trip went along, that it was wise to add about fifteen minutes to any appointed time; it seemed to be built into the system. If someone was going to meet you, he would arrive about fifteen minutes after the designated time; if an event was scheduled for a particular hour, it would start at least fifteen minutes after that. The exceptions were people working at the U.S. Embassy in Madrid, and Pablo Somarriba, who was a model of punctuality.)

We didn't talk much, since the driver knew no English. George started working on his extremely rusty Spanish out loud, with the driver correcting his pronunciation of certain words. Barcelona is a city of contrasts, and we rode from narrow medieval streets into wider, modern boulevards. A lot of rebuilding went on before the 1992 Olympics, and a lot is still going on. Barcelona, I discovered, attracts a lot of architects and students of architecture; with its variety of styles, including the moderniste style of Gaudí's structures, it's been called an architect's paradise. The Institute is on Barcelona's Via Augusta, one of the newer and more fashionable streets, and is housed in an eight-story building with classrooms, conference centers, and galleries for displays.

We were ushered into the lobby. An elevator took us up to an auditorium that also had a conference area in the back with chairs, a bar, and a balcony overlooking the Via Augusta.

Esther Gelabert of the Institute met us as we left the elevator. Esther had been faxing me at frequent intervals, since she had been handling most of the details of my trip. She was delighted to meet me! She hoped I was comfortable! At first glance, Esther looked rather plain, a youngish woman with long straight brown hair, a round, friendly moon-pie face, and glasses. I stopped thinking of her as plain about five minutes after I met her. For one thing, she had a great deal of warmth and a lovely voice. For another, like many of the people I was to see in Barcelona, she had a sense of style. However casually

---

ABOUT THE INSTITUTE

The Institute of North American Studies ("Instituto de Estudios Norteamericanos" in Spanish; "Institut d'Estudis Nordamericans" in Catalan) was founded in the 1950s by prominent Catalans who had studied in the United States and who much admired American culture. One thing they particularly admired was American democracy, something sorely missing in Spain during the years of the Franco dictatorship. Barcelona, which had been a hotbed of Communists and anarchists during the 1930s, and a center of resistance to Franco's forces until the bitter end of Spain's Civil War, had especially suffered under the Franco regime. The Catalan language was banned, and Catalan culture suppressed. In the 1970s, after Franco's death, the Institute moved to its present quarters, which were constructed with the help of a loan from the U.S. government. Since then, the Institute has sponsored many cultural exchange programs and conducted classes in the English language and American literature. The goal of the Institute is, in its words, to "serve as a bridge between the people of North America and Catalunya."

people in this city were dressed (and they tend to be relatively informal), they never looked like slobs. If you were a woman, a dress was never out of place no matter where you went. (During the days I was in Barcelona, the only people I ever saw in T-shirts, shorts, or athletic shoes were Americans or, more rarely, teenaged Barcelonians. Barcelona women wearing jeans almost always wore leather shoes, heels, or often stylish ankle-high boots. Men, even if they weren't wearing ties, usually wore sports jackets or suits.)

Pablo was already there, presiding over the bottles of mineral water lining the bar. He asked me if I had slept well; I told him that I had slept like a log. "I hope," he added, "that the noise didn't bother you." What noise? I wanted to know. "Phil Collins's press conference," he said. "He's staying at Le Meridien. He had a press conference in the lobby last night. It was a mob!" And here I had always thought of myself as a light sleeper.

I was introduced then to Elvira Saiz, the young woman who would be my interpreter. Elvira was small and slight, with short brown hair. She greeted me in a voice that could have come from Masterpiece Theatre. "You're British!" George exclaimed. "No, I'm Spanish," Elvira replied in her British accent. And, as I was to learn, many Spanish people who speak English speak it with a British accent and usage—not surprising, since England is closer than the States, many learned their English there, and Spain is flooded with British tourists in the summer.

Pablo had brought newly bound copies of my novel to give to reporters. He had made sure that all the journalists got unbound copies of my book, and pages of publicity about me and my research, although he confessed in apologetic-sounding tones that some of the reporters might not have read the whole novel, or only skimmed it. I told him I understood and that we had all too many reporters and reviewers like that in the US. "You will probably hear a lot of the same questions," Pablo said. I nodded, already guessing what some of them might be. "I don't worry about that so much," I admitted. "What I worry about is that I'll end up giving the same answers over and over and get sick of listening to myself." Repeat the same answer often enough, and pretty soon you sound like a politician giving canned, rehearsed answers at a press conference.

Alex Salmón of *El Mundo* was going to be late, according to Pablo, so my first interviewer was Asunción Guardia of *La Vanguardia*, one of the biggest papers in Spain and one of the most popular in Barcelona. Asunción Guardia was a middle-aged woman with reddish hair and, as it happened, the only woman, except for one television reporter later in the trip, to interview me. Apparently the Spanish cultural beat was dominated by men; in fact, women writers in Spain were still uncommon. Literature, it seemed, was basically a man's world.

I now had to adjust to the weird experience of speaking through an interpreter. If I said too much at once, Elvira was going to have more trouble remembering it all; saying too little, or keeping my sentences short, would make me sound like an idiot. I found myself speaking more slowly than usual and pausing between phrases so Elvira could translate before I went on. Pablo sat with me long enough to make sure I was handling myself well, then went off with George to talk in a corner.

Asunción Guardia had a lot of "women's" questions to ask me. How much influence did Genghis Khan's mother have on him? Most history is written by men; how is it different when seen through the eyes of women? And—my favorite—describe a typical day in the life of a Mongol woman. Ms. Guardia nodded sympathetically when I pointed out that Mongol men, except for making war, fashioning weapons, and herding sheep and horses, did little of the work around the camp. "Not much has changed!" she said. A photographer with her took pictures, hovering over me as I sat in a chair.

The *La Vanguardia* reporter had interviewed me for about forty minutes. The tardy Alex Salmón showed up next, asking questions I was to hear again later from others. Why did you want to write a book about Genghis Khan? What kind of research did you do? How long did it take you to write the book? Those sorts of questions.

It was nearly 11:00 when this interview was over. Somebody named Manuel Calderón from a newspaper called *ABC* was supposed to show up then; we waited. After about twenty minutes, Pablo, looking distinctly pissed off, picked up the phone behind the bar and called the *ABC* offices. As he was trying to find out what had happened, George and Elvira had the kind of discussion only multilingual people can have. "Do you think in Spanish when you're translating into English," George asked, "or do you think in English, too?" "In Spanish," Elvira admitted, "but I'm trying to think more in English." George confessed that in recent years, he tended to think in English even when he spoke in Polish, although as a child he had thought in Polish when speaking that language. "But I don't remember ever thinking in Polish," George finished, "when I was speaking in English." I brooded about how far I was from ever being able to think in French, let alone express a complex thought easily in that language.

Nobody at the *ABC* offices knew what had happened to the *ABC* reporter, but Pablo no longer seemed worried about that. "He should have been here," he said, "this is very rude, but it isn't that important. The next two reporters—they're the most important. They're *all* important, of course, but these two are the *most* important. One is from Agencia Efe, and the other is from *El País*." Efe was the main Spanish news agency, and *El País* the most important newspaper in Spain. These two guys, Pablo told me, had read my novel in its entirety, were experts on historical fiction, and were likely to ask me more challenging questions than the other reporters.

Great, I thought; now I can really start getting nervous. "Are they really going to grill me?" I asked. Are they going to come on like Mike Wallace on *60 Minutes*, I was thinking. "Oh, no," Pablo replied. "They will be kind. Do not worry!"

The journalist from Agencia Efe, Santos Romero, did not look like a kind-hearted man. He was a compact, dark-haired, bearded man with the air of a college professor—the kind of arrogant and impatient professor who throws students out of the classroom for asking stupid questions. Instead of asking me why I had written a novel about Genghis Khan, or what interested me in the subject, he asked me what had made me think I *could* write a novel about Genghis Khan, as if this might be beyond anyone's capacities. But none of his other questions were particularly hard, I fielded them easily, and he snapped his notebook shut and left after about twenty minutes. He was, I thought, about the coldest person I'd met in Spain so far.

The man from *El País*, Jacinto Antón, was entirely different. He was young and handsome and friendly! He loved my book! He was so enthusiastic about it that pretty soon Elvira, who was having trouble keeping up with us, had to ask us to slow down. And, about ten minutes into the interview, he asked the question that convinced me he was really smart.

That question was: "For your research, did you read Mircea Eliade's *Shamanism*?"

I had not mentioned Eliade and his study *Shamanism: Archaic Techniques of Ecstasy* in the short essay Pablo had translated, because there I had listed only primary sources. And Eliade is not an obvious secondary source for a book like *Ruler of the Sky*, because he was doing a study of Central Asian and Siberian shamanism in general, and not Mongolian shamanism in particular. I could have written my novel without reading Eliade's sometimes dense book, but some instinct had told me I'd better check his study out. If I was going to write about people to whom shamanism was so central, who perceived the world in shamanistic terms, who saw illness as an affliction of evil spirits, saw rocks, mountains, rivers, and other natural phenomena as inhabited by spirits, and who believed that shamans could speak to the spirits and even to the dead, I'd better have a good idea of what shamanism was all about. Eliade's study was *the* anthropological text on the subject. Even if I weren't writing overtly about shamanism, what I learned would provide an additional layer for the novel.

So I said to Jacinto Antón: "Of course I read Eliade."

He was delighted. Now he knew that I hadn't assumed that writing historical fiction was simply a matter of getting the facts straight and the details right, that I knew it required getting into the mentality of the people. After that, I was home free. He asked some of the same questions others had asked, one of them being how a writer of science fiction had become interested in writing a historical novel, and I soon discovered that he knew something about my other writing, too. He talked to me longer than any of the other journalists, for over an hour, and finally brought things to a halt only because his photographer needed time to shoot me, and another journalist, Javier Gafarot of *Diario 16*, had arrived.

I don't remember much about this interview, because by then it was well past two in the afternoon, Esther Gelabert had come back upstairs from her office for a moment, and everybody's mind (including, I suspect, Mr. Gafarot's) was on lunch. We were going to have to have a quick lunch, too, according to Pablo (a quick lunch in this context meaning one that lasts only an hour or an hour and a half instead of two hours or more), because the last journalist was to interview me at four. The *Diario 16* photographer followed us down the block and took pictures of me in a small park, where a gray-bearded man who was obviously drunk wandered over and tried to get his photo taken with me, before we headed off to a nearby restaurant Esther had recommended to us.

Pablo was in good spirits. He was relieved, I eventually found out, because he had been worrying about how I would handle the interviews. Specifically, he had been extremely worried that, because I had written science fiction and some of my scheduled speeches were about that subject (some of my other hosts had requested that I talk about science fiction, so I couldn't refuse to do so), *Ruler of the Sky* and historical fiction in general might get short shrift. As far as he was concerned, I was there primarily to promote that book, and if I didn't, it would be "a disaster," as he had told me in his last fax before my departure for Spain. Well, I felt exactly the same way, and central to all my speeches and interviews was my assertion that science fiction and historical fiction were related genres. At this point, I might as well steal some lines from a couple of my speeches:

...the best historical novelists may offer important insights into the past. What they can do is put the reader inside the minds of people of the past, show us their inner lives, make us feel what it would have been like to live them. This is also what the best writers of science fiction do—give the reader a "lived-in" future world, one that is more than the extrapolations of futurists or the statistical projections of economists, environmentalists, technologists, or doomsayers. In both cases, the writer must create a world bound by certain facts. In writing of the future, the writer is bound by what we know about the physical universe, the plausibility of future events and changes, what technological developments are likely, and how people might change, adapt, and live in these environments. In writing of the past, the writer has to keep in mind what has actually happened, what kinds of lives people are known to have led, what ideas they had about the world they lived in, what they thought of as being real. And, within the limits of these facts, the writer has to imagine the past or the future, but that imagination has to be rooted in reality.

And, in both cases, the writer must write about a world unlike his own, a world that can often be completely alien...

...To quote a colleague of mine, the American science fiction writer Kim Stanley Robinson: "It is possible to write historical fiction for the same reason one writes science fiction; to take advantage of the psychological power of the estrangement effect, which in pulling readers momentarily out of their ordinary world views, gives them the chance to see things anew."

So Pablo no longer had to worry. Whatever I talked about, *Ruler of the Sky* was going to be central to the discussion.

We had found out more about Pablo before lunch. As it turned out, he was also an American by birth—a Central American. Born in Costa Rica, he had grown up in the Panama Canal Zone, a place he remembers as a paradise—"my California," he called it. He became a big fan of American movies. As a young man, he studied anthropology at the University of Mexico, expecting that anthropology would be his profession. Just as he was finishing his graduate work, the Mexican government made drastic cuts in funding for the social sciences, meaning no jobs. He went to Paris and then Spain, where he quickly landed his job at Edhasa, where he had been for several years now. "And what a great job!" Esther had said.

For lunch, I followed Pablo's lead and ordered salad and a sturdy Catalan dish--a spicy bean soup with shellfish (clams, shrimp, mussels—you name it, with the clams still in their shells). We had begun the meal by demolishing plates of olives. (I was never an olive fan before, but Spain changed that; never have I enjoyed such a variety of tasty olives—black ones, green ones, olives that looked more like grapes, olives stuffed with capers or anchovies.) What a great feed! By now, I was well on the way to mastering an important Spanish vocabulary word, gambas, which means shrimp. George and Elvira dined on tiny little grilled lamb chops that looked as though they had come from miniature lambs. We drank wine and mineral water with the food, then ordered dessert (a pastry-like cake with fruit in my case) and coffee. This was where I discovered that coffee after meals, generally speaking, is a separate course in itself. You can ask to have it served with dessert, and some people do, but usually Spaniards finish the dessert first and then have the coffee, sometimes with a liqueur. It's also, as I had found out that morning at breakfast, very strong coffee (although much better coffee, in my relatively uninformed opinion, than Italian or French coffee) so I always had it *con leche*—with milk. The milk is almost always warm milk.

So we ate well, and talked, and did a post-mortem of sorts on the interviews. Pablo wanted to know if we'd like to do some sightseeing with him after the last interview, and we quickly said yes.

About five minutes after we got back to the Institute (we were at least ten minutes late), Carlos Vatbueno of *El Periódico* showed up; the fifteen-minutes-late rule was still holding. I don't remember much about this interview except that Mr. Vatbueno was yet another handsome young man (Spanish journalism seems to have a high percentage of such guys), and he was the only journalist who used a tape recorder; everyone else had brought notebooks and written everything down.

It had been a long day. I scoped out the front of the large room, the auditorium in which I would give my first speech the next night, and decided not to get nervous just yet. Esther Gelabert gave me extra copies of both the publicity for my speech, an elegantly designed bilingual invitation in Spanish on one side and Catalan on the other, and the brochure about the Institute program of which I was a part, the fifth year of their North American Writers Series.

They had invited five writers that year. William Kennedy was the first, and I was the last.

* * * *

Esther had promised to take us sightseeing the next day, on visits to Gaudí's La Pedrera and La Sagrada Família Cathedral, but our Gaudí experience for today would be a walk in the Parc Güell, where we went by taxi.

Along the walkways that crisscross Güell Park are stone arches that almost look as though they are melting. The weather had cleared up that afternoon, and we had some sunshine for our stroll. It's difficult to describe this park. While you're in it, you feel as though you're completely inside a brilliant eccentric's mind; the place looks like nothing else on earth. One area of the park is a huge disk of sand, on which people can stroll or sit, supported by tall stone pillars that aren't quite straight. Along one stairway, a brightly painted dragon is a fountain, spewing water from its jaws. Stony recesses and caves line another path leading away from the pillars.

This phantasmagorical park was where Pablo's ten-year-old daughter usually came to play with her friends after school. His apartment was in the neighborhood of narrow streets and balconied houses below the hill on which the park is located, and his daughter's school was nearby. What a great place for a kid, I thought. "She's going to look at the world really differently," George said, "spending her formative years in this spot. This is weird imprinting." "She will be an architect!" Pablo said. And my feeling is that anybody growing up in Barcelona probably has a leg up in that profession.

We wandered in this wonderland for at least an hour, probably more, before taking a taxi back to the central part of the city. The Spanish government was, it seems, going through a major scandal, which Pablo was soon discussing with the cabdriver. The head of the Bank of Spain, their equivalent of the head of the Federal Reserve,

---

ABOUT ANTONI GAUDÍ

Born in 1852, Antoni Gaudí i Cornet was to become Barcelona's most famous and controversial architect. The Parc Güell (Güell Park) was built for one of his most important patrons, the industrialist Eusebi Güell. Gaudí specialized in bizarre, strange shapes—he was a lover of forests—and Güell Park is full of mushroom shapes and other natural shapes; many of the columns and supports for structures in the park are shaped like flowers or fungi. After many romantic affairs, Gaudí became increasingly religious and decided that he "lacked the aptitude for a family life." His work is all over Barcelona, sprouting like strange natural growths in the middle of urban development. He died in 1926, after being run over by a tram; he was in the middle of work on La Sagrada Família Cathedral, which remains unfinished. Penniless, as he usually was, he had been living in his workroom at the cathedral and habitually wore ragged and dirty clothing, which is why he lay unrecognized in a pauper's ward for a few days at the hospital where he finally died. All of Barcelona turned out for his funeral, and he was buried in a crypt at his unfinished cathedral.

had just resigned after admitting to having stolen millions of pesetas from the treasury. Spaniards, we were discovering, were completely mystified as to why Americans (and the British) got so worked up about sexual shenanigans on the part of politicians; that kind of thing didn't matter. "Money," Pablo said, "that is important!" That was worth getting upset about. (And, as news about Bill Clinton and his accuser Paula Jones made its way across the Atlantic, the Spanish seemed even more mystified by the fuss Americans made over such matters. To them, Ms. Jones's allegations were of no importance, and had nothing to do with a person's fitness to hold office, even if they were true.)

We got out of the cab several blocks from the Plaça Catalunya and took a walk past another Gaudí structure, La Pedrera, which has to qualify as one of the most bizarre apartment buildings in the history of the world. Gaudí was commissioned to build it for the Milás, another of Barcelona's wealthy families; they had only the vaguest idea of how the building would look and were allegedly horrified when they finally saw the completed structure. The stone along the sides of the building twists and turns at each level, and the roof is lined by structures that look like helmeted soldiers. The inside lobby looks more like a big cave than the entrance to a building. Esther, Pablo told us, would try to get us to the roof of La Pedrera tomorrow, although she would have to pull strings to do it, since visitors weren't allowed there.

We caught a bus to the Plaça Catalunya. By "bus" I mean a small, quiet, extremely comfortable vehicle that seated about sixteen people and made short hops; there were larger buses and streetcars for longer distances, and a subway system as well, plus the taxis, which are generally cheap. I was beginning to realize that, even with Barcelona's confusing layout of streets (the buildings in L'Eixample, the most modern-looking part of town, aren't numbered, and the streets in the Barri Gótic are a maze), we probably wouldn't get permanently lost. At worst, we could always find a bus headed for the Plaça Catalunya, since it was such a central spot, or get a cab to take us there, and the hotel was just a few minutes down the street from the Plaça.

George, scoping out the passers-by, made the observation that the young people of Barcelona, although openly affectionate, seemed more restrained and decorous in their amorous public displays than

American teenagers. (After I got back to the States, our friend Warren Wagar, a professor and historian who had been in Barcelona during the 1960s, told me that back then, the police would harass and arrest couples caught kissing in public. That's how repressive Franco's regime was, and maybe the habit of restraint still holds because of that.) Pablo left us at one end of the Plaça Catalunya, where he could easily find a bus or cab home. We headed toward the Café Zurich, a sidewalk café on La Rambla and across from the Plaça where you can sit at an outside table and order a beer, which is exactly what we did. It's said that, if you sit there long enough, no matter where in the world you're from, someone you know will walk by sooner or later. It's also a popular hangout for journalists. We didn't run into anyone we knew, but sat there for much of the early evening enjoying our beer.

Pablo called after we got back to the hotel. He had managed to find a copy of the Spanish edition of the anthology *Foundation's Friends,* a tribute to Isaac Asimov composed of stories set in backgrounds derived from Asimov's fiction by several notable science fiction writers (called *Asimov y sus amigos* in Spanish), and promised to give it to me the next day, since George and I each had a story in the book. I was delighted he had found one, that he had taken the trouble to buy the book for us.

We also found out later what Le Meridien's customary nighttime service was, and it was provided to us every night during our stay. When we came back to our room at night, the covers on the bed were always turned down, bottled mineral water, glasses, and a small box of chocolates for each of us sat on the night tables, and my nightgown and George's pajamas were always folded and arranged neatly on the bed. They would even put our hotel terrycloth slippers on top of mats on either side of the bed, so that our dainty little feet would never have to touch the carpeting. I'm surprised they didn't come by later to tuck us in.

Barcelona is a romantic city. At least I found it so, in early May, before the really hot weather sets in. We could lounge around in Le Meridien's big terrycloth bathrobes drinking cava on the outside balcony while gazing out over the rooftops, and then go inside after the sun set to think about dinner. At this point, as the Victorian novelists used to do, I will close the curtain on this scene.

But before doing that, I'll mention George's momentous discovery. After soaking in the tub, he decided that his ankle-high black boots needed shining. The hotel had a complimentary shoe-shining service; if you put your shoes outside your door before midnight, they would be returned to you shined by five in the morning. George put his boots into the large wooden box the hotel provided and, clothed only in his towel, opened the door to put them in the hallway.

At that moment, Phil Collins, with a woman who might have been his wife or his girlfriend, walked by. George looked at him and Phil Collins gazed back calmly, as if seeing a guy in a towel putting his shoes in the hallway was a fairly normal sight to him. "Holy shit," George said after he closed the door. "Phil Collins is in the room next door."

Here's another difference between five-star hotels and other hotels: You can't hear the sounds in other rooms. Not once were we disturbed by anyone else's noise. And, judging by the empty bottles and room service trays I saw outside Phil Collins's door the next morning, I'm guessing he threw a party.

THURSDAY, MAY 5, 1994

We got up late; I knew I would have to be at my best that evening, so it didn't seem worthwhile to get up so early that I'd be exhausted by the time of my speech. We wandered down to breakfast at about nine-thirty, or maybe later. Godzilla and her associate were nowhere in evidence, but there were a lot of scruffy-looking young British guys who looked like musicians or roadies; I figured they were part of Phil Collins's entourage. I had the odd sensation that a few other people were staring at me for some reason, and worried that maybe I shouldn't have washed my hair the night before; it had gone completely big and wild on me.

The day before, we had heard from Pablo that his wife, Henriette Somarriba Hubacher, was a literary agent with an agency that had branches in Buenos Aires and Mexico City as well as in Barcelona. Maybe we would have a chance to get someone to represent us directly in Spain. "The literary agents are all women!" Pablo had said. Well, at least one aspect of Spain's literary life was dominated by women.

Occasionally somebody at the Institute would fax the hotel an updated itinerary for me. The latest one indicated that I would be giving my speech at the Institute at 7:00 PM, to be followed by dinner, and my lecture at the University of Barcelona on Friday was still scheduled for eleven (it turned out to be closer to noon), followed by lunch.

Here, I'll digress for a moment.

SOME COMMENTARY

One of my father's pet peeves was being asked to speak or sing before some group, and having to eat his meal before the performance. We had discussions about this several times. "Why, when people and organizations invite you to speak," I asked him, "do they insist on feeding you beforehand? You can't enjoy the meal, because you're nervous about the speech or whatever, and you have to worry about eating certain things because they might interfere with your performance." Dad was of one mind with me about that; he couldn't understand it, either, and it could be even more of a problem for a singer. Certain foods can clog your voice, or make you belch. You want to have a couple of drinks to steady your nerves, but then worry that the booze might affect the clarity of your speech. On one occasion, at the University at Albany, I was served a meal of Mexican food, tacos and burritos and such, before I was to give a reading; I ended up at the podium rasping from thirst and hoping the beans wouldn't give me audible gas. "They should let you go on first," Dad would say, "and then give you your chow." But in the United States, they practically never do.

This was never an issue in Spain. Everybody eats meals so late there by American standards—I noticed this in my schedule immediately—that you never have to endure a meal before your public performance. You can enjoy it afterward, to the full, and savor it in a relaxed state of mind.

I am now convinced, after my Spanish experience, that the treatment of invited speakers and guests by groups in the US is often barbaric. If I were going to recommend anything to people inviting a speaker or other performer, I would say: "Offer the speaker a choice. Tell him you'll be happy to take him out after the speech, even if it's really late. Or, if it's one of those big banquet deals, promise that the caterer won't start serving the food, not even the salad, until he's finished his presentation. A lot of people will be delighted to take you up on the offer."

This means it may take you longer to eat, and you may have to allot more time for the event, but so what? Another habit of the Spanish I much admired was their willingness to take their time at meals, to enjoy the food and the conversation, not to have to go rushing around frantically. I mean, exactly what are all these Americans eating their fifteen and twenty-minute lunches and half-hour dinners rushing to do?

* * * *

We took a walk after breakfast. It seemed like a good day to orient ourselves by wandering around, and Esther would be by that afternoon to take us sightseeing, and then we would go directly to the Institute. That meant I'd have to wear my glad rags and be dressed up during the sightseeing, but I didn't mind that. I was getting used to walking around in a dress, instead of my usual garb of jeans and Reeboks, and the weather was at that perfect temperature, around 70 degrees Fahrenheit or slightly higher, where a dress and stockings and dressy but comfortable shoes were the perfect wandering-around garb.

We took it easy. Basically, we wandered around the streets near the Plaça Catalunya, looked in stores, and ate an early lunch of salad at a sidewalk cafe. I didn't want to exhaust myself too much before the speech, the thought of which was making me more nervous as the hour grew closer.

We went back to the hotel, and Esther arrived not long afterward, around two-thirty, looking extremely chic in a green suit with a long straight skirt and matching suede shoes. The weather was turning out to be perfect. Esther figured we should take a cab over to La Pedrera first, and then go to La Sagrada Família, which lay closer to the Institute.

As we walked along La Rambla toward a cab stand, Esther had a sudden inspiration. "Let's check the papers," she said; we headed toward the nearest newsstand. Esther leafed through the papers. The man at the counter began to protest, obviously unhappy about someone looking through his wares who hadn't yet paid for them. Esther said something to him. "I told him," she said, "that you were a celebrated author and that there might be articles about you in the newspapers." She let out a cry as she came to the cultural section of *La Vanguardia*. "Here it is! They published the interview!" She rummaged through *El País* and emitted another cry. "And here, too!" She checked out the other papers, which hadn't published anything yet, then paid for the two that had run articles. "This is wonderful," Esther said, perusing the *El País* piece. "It's so well-written!" She explained to me that *El País* was the most widely-read newspaper, especially by intellectuals and people who read books, and that *La Vanguardia* was a close second in popularity. So I had done extremely, spectacularly well, she thought, in having pieces in both those papers out so soon; the other papers didn't matter nearly so much. "Pablo will be very happy!" she assured me.

I was pretty damned stunned. It had never even occurred to me to glance at the Spanish papers that day. Multiple copies of *El País*, *La Vanguardia*, and every other Spanish paper, along with the *International Herald Tribune* and various British, French, and German papers, were always available in Le Meridien's dining room for hotel guests to read during breakfast. They had been sitting there that very morning, while I was nursing my coffee and feeling relieved that Godzilla and her friend weren't around. I had thought, somewhat paranoically, that a few people at breakfast were looking at me funny. Maybe they had been reading *El País,* where the piece about me was on a page next to one with an article about Clint Eastwood. I had achieved the Spanish equivalent of having a big write-up in the *New York Times*.

We took a cab over to La Pedrera. We got to see this bizarre but wonderful building close up, including the cave-like lobby, but the people in charge weren't letting anybody onto the elevators, which were problematic and needed repairs, to go up to the roof. Absolutely *nobody*. Esther tried to pull some strings, telling them that I was a noted personage and this would be my only chance to go up to the roof, but nothing worked. "Don't worry about it," I told Esther when we left. "This just gives me another excuse to come back to Barcelona another time." I had accumulated a number of reasons for a return visit already.

We went by cab to La Sagrada Família, which has to be one of the best-known Barcelona landmarks. It was still unfinished, and likely to remain so until well after the year 2000, although people were out on the street collecting money for the construction and restoration. (It is now scheduled to be completed in 2026.) Gaudí died in the midst of work on this cathedral, and then the Civil War came (the people of Barcelona managed to keep this cathedral and the old Gothic cathedral from being destroyed during a bout of anti-clerical rioting and violence in 1936, when almost every other church in the city was burned or bombed), and then construction proceeded without people being quite sure of what the finished structure should look like.

The place is as strange and eerie as I expected. George and I stood around studying the west entrance while Esther went off to make a phone call to the Institute about some last-minute business. Above this entrance are huge angular stone figures, sculpted by Josep

Maria Subirachs and the subject of some controversy. (The fact that the sculptor Subirachs was an atheist didn't exactly ease the minds of some people.) The figures depict the scenes shown in the Stations of the Cross; the Roman soldiers look as though they could have come from a science fiction movie, and the figure of Christ on the cross is completely nude. Above all of this rise the almost impossibly slender spires of the cathedral.

When Esther got back, we walked around to the other side, the east entrance, to study the structure. It's the perfect example of something that shouldn't work, that shouldn't move the viewer, but does. To describe it is to make it sound almost tacky. All that weird ornate carved stuff on the sides! Big white stone doves with painted green olive branches in their beaks! Big pink letters spelling out "Sanctus, Sanctus," on the side of one spire! Still, it overwhelmed me. George said, "It almost makes me feel as if I should go to confession."

We went back to the western side to pay our admission. Inside, an elevator would take us up to a bridge between the slender spires, where we could get a bird's-eye view of the city. Esther was a little worried that we might have trouble getting the elevator; several tour buses were parked out front. Miraculously, we had the elevator practically to ourselves. You get off the elevator, climb a narrow flight of steps between stone walls so close on both sides that you feel they're going to press in on you (George later admitted that this climb gave him the creeps), and come out finally on the narrow stone span. All of Barcelona is visible; you can see it clear to the Mediterranean. You also get a great view, needless to say, of the unfinished cathedral from above. Still, it isn't a sight for anyone prone to claustrophobia or fear of heights. George, standing on that stone bridge and looking at how slim the stone towers are, was only too conscious, as he put it, that the whole thing had been designed by essentially an amateur architect, one who had proceeded largely by trial and error. He was wondering what would happen if any cracks developed.

At last we left and went across the street to have sodas and study La Sagrada Família from another angle; it's the kind of place you don't want to leave too quickly.

We took another cab over to the Institute; I wanted to get there at least half an hour early. Esther caught up on the political situation with the cabdriver. The head of Spain's National Guard had disappeared with millions of pesetas. The vice-premier had resigned, apparently admitting that he had helped to ravage the treasury. This was big-time corruption, not penny-ante Congressman Dan Rostenkowski-type misdeeds.

Before going upstairs to the auditorium, Esther showed us around the Institute's library and introduced us to a young woman named Dina, one of the librarians. People came to this library all the time to borrow books in English, since the Institute's main purpose is to promote the study of American language and culture. Unfortunately, a lot of funding once provided by the U.S. government had been frozen, so the library was having trouble buying books. They especially had trouble with science fiction, very popular among borrowers, because it was hard to figure out which books to buy; no one could keep up with the field. George and I realized immediately that a lot of writers we knew would be happy to send copies of their books to the Institute, and got information as to how to go about it. (After returning home, we contacted several sf writers about this and contributed some of our own books.)

As for my invitation, Dina told me more about the steps that had led up to it. The Institute works with Spanish publishers to decide on and invite American writers. A publisher would come to John Zvereff, the head of the Institute, and propose inviting a particular writer (Pablo had presented my name for consideration). The Institute then had to decide whether this writer was someone they wanted there, at which point the librarian, in this case Dina, goes through slews of reference works to gather information about the writer. Once the publisher and the Institute are set on a particular writer, the U.S. Information Service at the embassy in Madrid gets into the act—which is, basically, how my trip grew.

And if the Institute had decided I wasn't interesting or important enough to invite, the whole process would have ended there, and I wouldn't have gone to Spain.

Pablo was waiting upstairs, along with the person who was to introduce me. She was Dolors Bramon, a professor at the University of Barcelona and an Islamic scholar. (There was an irony in this, as Dr. Bramon quickly pointed out, since the Islamic documents dealing with Genghis Khan were all written by people the Mongols had conquered and those texts had contributed to their bad historical reputation.) She had dark hair and exotic eye makeup; she was also a heavy smoker, and I was struck by the fact that she could puff away on her cigarettes without the nonsmokers in the vicinity jumping down her throat. John Zvereff, the Institute's Executive Director, was with her; he turned out to be a tall, good-looking blond man of Russian heritage. He was, in fact, the child of diplomats; he had been born in Rome, grown up there and in other European cities, and spoke fluent Spanish and Catalan after years in Barcelona. Although he is an American citizen, the only time he ever actually lived in the U.S. was when he was going to college at Georgetown University.

We chatted for a while; Dr. Bramon's daughter, who was fluent in English and had studied at Princeton, was with her, and made me promise to send copies of my Venus books to her. The interpreter who was to translate my speech simultaneously into Spanish took me aside for a pow-wow. She had a copy of my speech—I'd given one to Esther to photocopy for her—but was worried about what to do when I read passages from my novel. I showed her which passages I intended to read, and we located them in the Spanish edition; luckily the chapter numbers are the same in both editions, even if the page numbers aren't.

And then it was time to face my audience—about twenty minutes later than the announced time.

Esther had told me that Spanish audiences are shy. I was to hear this everywhere I went in that country. Spanish audiences are quiet and don't ask questions; don't feel strange if nobody asks you anything. Also, for some reason, the speaker is usually seated behind a table, which I found a bit disorienting, instead of standing at a podium. The person who introduces you always sits next to you during the speech, and often will be the first to get the ball rolling on questions afterward. On top of that, I was equipped with an earpiece through which I could listen to a simultaneous translation of Dolors Bramon's introduction, and was careful to make sure I didn't spill my bottled water in front of everybody while pouring it into my glass.

There the audience was, listening as John Zvereff introduced both me and Dr. Bramon. George was way in the back, because he didn't want me distracted by his presence. (He was to follow this modus operandi at every speech.) What a relief to hear Dr. Bramon, who had read my novel thoroughly, talk about my command of the source material! And then it was time for me to talk.

The title of the speech was "The Historical Novelist and History." A lot of it was about how I had gone about the process of writing *Ruler of the Sky*. I have found over the years that most people, for some reason, like to hear about the process of writing. To me, it sometimes seems about as interesting as listening to a recital of a trade manual, combined with tales of psychological hangups and inspirational advice, but it is almost always a sure-fire topic for most audiences. I ranged pretty far afield in this presentation, bringing in the connections between science fiction and historical fiction and how the Mongols' warrior ethos resembles that of urban street gangs. I picked two different passages to read from my novel, one a battle scene and the other a confrontation between Genghis Khan and his mother.

It all went over! They actually liked it! I didn't get any questions (Esther was right about that), but no one looked bored, and Pablo thought my choice of readings was so inspired that he planned to use the excerpts I'd chosen in future publicity. One weird guy came up and thrust a note with various questions into my hand (I still have the letter), but didn't seem to want me to answer them there. Esther was full of praise: "That was brilliant," she said, "and that's not a word I use lightly." She was particularly taken with the stuff about the process of writing.

And I was tremendously relieved, because screwing up on that speech would have spooked me for the rest of the trip. I would have been trying to make up for it and probably working myself into a state of total panic.

* * * *

I don't recall the name of the restaurant where we went to dinner, but wish I did, because it was a great place, with big tables and linen tablecloths and napkins and a formal but comfortable atmosphere and great food.

We sat down at our table at about nine-thirty, a normal dinner hour, even a bit early, by Spanish standards. Pablo was cheerful. Now he knew I wouldn't completely disgrace him. John Zvereff was ordering drinks. He was having a gin and tonic, and so was George, and

I decided to reward myself with a martini. This caused some trouble for the waiter, who didn't know how to make one. "It's okay," I said, "a gin and tonic will be fine." "Oh, no," John insisted. A martini was a standard drink, and there was no reason why I shouldn't have one. The waiter, after making one with the help of instructions from John, seemed happy to add this drink to his repertoire. (This was, however, the only time I had a cocktail in Spain, because the Spanish, like a lot of Europeans, drink mostly beer and wine; hard liquor is not the usual thing.)

As for the food, it was great. Pablo talked me into trying a salad made with red peppers, and I had paella, a rice and sea food dish flavored with saffron and with loads of gambas (and considered a classic Spanish dish) for the main course. And we drank wine and talked, a lot, about almost everything. George, careful to phrase the remark so that it was clear it wasn't *his* opinion, allowed as how some people claimed that Franco, despite being a dictator, had at least kept the peace in Spain for the thirty years after World War II. "The peace of death," Pablo replied in a gloomy voice. John was almost relieved to hear horror stories from us (considerably toned down, in the interest of being diplomatic) about publishing and the general wretched state of middle management in the U.S. "I thought," he said after recounting some of his own difficulties with the Institute's Board of Directors (who seemed prone to tell John to try projects that he had already been doing for years), "that my problems might be unique." Now he had yet more evidence that the stupidity in human organizations is endemic. Most of us had crema Catalana for dessert, which is something like a cross between a Creme Brulée and a flan, and followed that with coffee and a colorless liqueur that was too powerful to drink in anything but tiny sips. I got to sign the Institute's guest book, which was an experience in itself, since the pages were filled with famous signatures. There was Joyce Carol Oates, and Allen Ginsberg, and William Kennedy ("thanks for inviting a guy to Barcelona to talk about Albany"), and slews of others. How the hell did I get there?

We left at around midnight, and people were still in the restaurant eating. In that contented frame of mind, I could almost forget that I had to give another speech the next day.

FRIDAY, MAY 6, 1994

Pablo, as always, was on time in the morning. The University of Barcelona was just around the corner, so to speak, and I could cash my Institute check and get some pesetas at a bank along the way. I was to speak to a large group of English-language graduate students, and would be introduced by Professor Angels Carabi.

I was to speak in the Aula Magna, a huge room with high ceilings and a row of tall wooden chairs, carved and lined with purple cushions, in the front of the room behind a long table. It looked more as though I'd be holding court instead of speaking. The Aula Magna was housed in a building new by Spanish standards—it was about a hundred and fifty years old. A wide staircase beyond a huge arched doorway led to the second floor, where I was to lecture, and on the stairs and in the hallways were young people in white uniforms, aprons, and chef's hats, standing rigidly at attention. It turned out, by coincidence, that a huge celebration of Catalan cuisine was being held at the university; chefs had come there from all over Catalunya.

We waited, Pablo and George and I, by the door to the Aula Magna. Unfortunately, Professor Carabi, John Zvereff, and a couple of other people were waiting for us in the courtyard below. This is why, when someone finally came looking for us, I was about half an hour late in starting my speech instead of the usual fifteen to twenty minutes.

Angels Carabi was an extremely pretty woman with an oval face and curly black hair. She was also an ardent feminist and fan of the *Women of Wonder* anthologies, and thus delighted to learn that I was working on new *WoW* volumes. Clutching a copy of the Spanish *Ruler of the Sky*, she asked me to autograph it. With her was an architect from California named Alex Meconi, who was a friend of one of Professor Carabi's graduate students; he had decided to come to my speech because it "sounded interesting." We went inside the hall, Professor Carabi introduced me to the audience in extremely flattering terms, and I gave a speech entitled "Science Fiction, Historical Fiction, and Alternative History." (I asked George afterward if it went well—he had been sitting way in the back with John and Pablo, where I couldn't see them—and he said that John had kept nudging him in the ribs and saying, "Hey, that's really good!" at certain points.) Despite the warnings about shy audiences, I got several questions, and might have had more if we hadn't run out of time.

John Zvereff extracted a promise from me to send him both of my speeches, since he was sure he could get them published in Spanish and Catalan. Pablo had to get back to his office, but was going to meet us next morning for some sightseeing. Angels Carabi apologized profusely for not having time to have lunch with me, and then she, George, Alex, Angels's grad student (who was writing a dissertation on Nathanael West) and I went downstairs to the courtyard and the celebration of Catalan cuisine. This was how I learned that, in Spain, when somebody tells you he doesn't have time for lunch (or dinner), what he means is that he doesn't have time to sit around for two and a half hours sharing a proper meal with you and isn't going to insult you by asking you to bolt your food in an hour or an hour and a half. Because Angels Carabi did have about an hour and a half to hang around with us in the courtyard before going to her next class, and of course there were all those Catalan treats to enjoy.

And there we were, talking and grazing on Catalan delicacies cooked by some of the best chefs in the country. The young people in white uniforms and chef's hats were moving among the knots of people with huge silver trays of food and wine. We didn't even have to go looking for the food and wine; about every five minutes, somebody would materialize near us and offer us something from a tray. Angels was doing balancing acts with her wine glass, her food, and her cigarettes. I ate tapas (appetizers) made of all kinds of sea food and little flat pastries that were like miniature pizzas. There were little sausages, and cheeses, and treats made with Jabon ham. I wasn't sure what some of the food was, but ate it anyway; you couldn't go wrong, since everything was good. We washed it all down with white wine, red wine, and sparkling wine.

Angels was fascinated, not surprisingly, by the importance of women writers in the U.S. She had recently become interested in some of the Native American writers, so we talked about Louise Erdrich, Paula Gunn Allen, and Leslie Marmon Silko, among others.

Alex was in Barcelona because, as an architect, that was the place to be. Much was being built, and the whole city was basically a course in different styles of architecture. Eventually we all had to go about our business, but not before George and I had accumulated more business cards and addresses so that we could keep in touch with everybody.

We walked back to the hotel, too stuffed to think about lunch. Esther had been unable to come to my speech, having a lot of work to catch up on, but had sent someone to the hotel with our airplane and train tickets for the rest of the trip. George wanted to get in a bit of rest before we went sightseeing; our plan was to go to Barcelona's Gothic cathedral, then to the Museo Picasso if there was time. It was then, back in our room, that we made a discovery.

May is the big bullfighting month in Spain, and during the last two weeks of the month, there are several bullfights a day. Bullfighting is more of a big deal in Madrid than in Barcelona, and it was apparently difficult, even for Spaniards, to get tickets to the big bullfights.

But, as it happens, you can watch the bullfights from Madrid on television. They show you the bull, who has a name and various statistics, including weight and lineage. Just before he goes into the ring, you see a guy sitting on the edge of the stall stab the bull in the back of the neck with what looks like a really mean spike. Then out the bull goes into the arena, where the picadors stab at him, and a guy on horseback goes after him, and eventually, when he's got a fair number of spikes in him and is clearly pissed off and in pain, or seemingly stunned into helplessness by all the torment, the matador dances around him with his red cape, kneeling and swirling the cape and otherwise daring the bull to gouge him before finally killing the bull with his sword. You get to see some of this stuff in slo-mo instant replays, too.

"You know something?" George said as we were watching one bullfight. "Lately I feel a lot like that bull."

* * * *

That evening, the street people were out in force, the mimes and beggars and pickpockets and all the rest. I kept a good grip on my purse, as I had been strongly advised to do by almost everyone since arriving. We finally, after one false start, found the broad street that would lead us directly to the Gothic cathedral. We passed some breakdancers surrounded by a crowd, a puppeteer dressed in a conductor's tails with a tiny orchestra of marionettes, a woman who sounded like a trained opera singer singing arias. Some of these people, along with the mimes, were the equivalent of panhandlers, but they were offering performances for their handouts.

The cathedral itself is some eight hundred years old, and stands overlooking a large square; there are Roman ruins and a Roman wall nearby. The central nave, with the altar, is so huge that it can be seen from almost anywhere inside the church. Saint Eulalia, Barcelona's patron saint, is supposedly buried here. Her story is a fairly gory and sadomasochistic one, as are many stories about saints in this part of the world; she was basically tortured by Romans (Barcelona was once a Roman city) for her Christian beliefs (I won't go into the grisly details) and eventually crucified. Unlike Gaudí's cathedral, which is largely the vision of one person, this church was built over the course of two centuries by masons, craftsmen, and others, and you can only wonder at the effort that went into it. Along the sides of the cathedral are various small chapels dedicated to Mary and other saints. In one, a woman was kneeling next to a life-sized Christ on the cross, kissing its feet as she prayed. There were other people praying in other places, and there seemed to be a mass going on in one chapel. With a few exceptions, most of the people praying (as opposed to those who were sightseers), were middle-aged or old.

We spent so much time exploring the cathedral that there was no time to get to the Museo Picasso before it closed at eight. No problem; we would have plenty of time to see it tomorrow. It was finally dawning on me that the pressure was off for a while, that I wouldn't have to give any speeches or interviews the next day.

In fact, all I'd have to do was enjoy myself.

SATURDAY, MAY 7, 1994

We went out to Montjuïc with Pablo in the morning. This is the huge hill—a mountain, really—that we could see from our hotel room. The Olympic stadium was built here, and we strolled past it while taking a walk along the tree-lined streets. It was a simple matter to take a cab to Montjuïc, even though it was more on the outskirts of the city. In fact, not only was it easy to get around without a car, a car would actually have gotten in the way. Parking is impossible, and the drivers speed a lot. You can't help thinking how much more pleasant American life would be if people didn't have to drive everywhere.

Pablo's custom was to go at least once a year to the Joan Miró Foundation on Montjuïc, a beautifully designed museum (the rooms are large and airy, with white walls and a lot of natural light) which has probably the largest Miró collection in the world. It also has one of the weirdest fountains I've ever seen, a Calder fountain with mercury instead of water flowing along its passages and into a bowl; the fountain, being toxic, is entirely enclosed by glass. Pablo wasn't quite sure what he thought of Miró, but something about the artist and the museum kept attracting him. I wasn't sure what I thought, either; Miró takes some getting used to. One piece that George and I stared at for a while was a huge tapestry of abstract shapes and colors covering one wall. Some of the sculptures, several labeled simply "Mujer" ("Woman"), with breasts that looked like penises, gave me pause. One of them had breasts that looked like lethal weapons. George reacted so strongly to this sculpture that he had hung his cane on one breast before realizing what he was doing. A guard came running, looking as if she was ready to kill George. Pablo was trying not to laugh. We're going to get thrown out, I thought. Somehow George managed to explain to the guard that the piece of art had had an extremely powerful effect on him, and she seemed to understand; he wasn't a vandal, only an art appreciator. Pablo was relieved—at least he wasn't going to have to bail us out of trouble—then told a story of how he had once been picked up in Mexico City on a trumped up loitering charge by the police.

(And, to be honest, I had the feeling that a person wouldn't want to run afoul of the police in Barcelona, either, or anywhere else in Spain. The occasional police I saw walking their beats looked tough, like the kinds of young guys who would hit you over the head with their truncheons and enjoy the procedure, if you gave them any guff. They resembled clean-cut versions of the gang members in *A Clockwork Orange*.)

We spent a lot of time with the Mirós, then checked out the museum's latest exhibit, which happened to be Robert Mapplethorpe's controversial display of photographs, the same display that had caused Senator Jesse Helms to rage against the National Endowment for the Arts and the Cincinnati Museum's director to be hauled into court for promoting obscenity when the photographs were on display in that city. Here people, including senior citizens and moms with babies and strollers, were wandering about without looking nonplussed. Why had some Americans made such a big deal about this exhibit? There was a fair amount of male nudity and some pretty graphic gay sadomasochistic stuff, and Mapplethorpe definitely liked photographing penises, especially big ones, but most of the pictures were fairly innocuous, portraits and flowers and the like. What struck me was how similar Mapplethorpe's lighting and technique was to that of our photographer pal Jay Kay Klein, although Jay Kay might not have appreciated the comparison.

Pablo delivered his verdict while standing in front of a group of photographs of big dicks. "This does not speak to me," he said solemnly. "It's technically proficient, but it does not speak to me."

From the museum, we took a cab down to the waterfront, at the other end of Barcelona. I was picking up vibes from Pablo at this point, and so was George. Pablo had been busting his ass on my behalf all week, besides keeping up with whatever other work he had to do. Saturday was a day off for him. It was moving on towards two in the afternoon. It was time to say farewell, even though I knew he would take us anywhere else we wanted to go; he was that kind of guy. So we walked along the harbor, and looked at the statue of Columbus in the square (he's pointing to America), and then we said we should probably go back to the hotel and get ready to head over to the

Museo Picasso, and Pablo protested, "Are you sure? Is there nothing else I can do?" and we assured him that he had been Mr. Wonderful in every respect.

He looked relieved. My guess is that he wanted to spend some time with his family.

We took a cab back to La Rambla and said our farewells there. Pablo explained that I wouldn't have to look through the Sunday papers for any more articles about myself; unlike U.S. papers, Spanish ones don't have literary supplements on Sundays. "On Sundays," Pablo explained, "people just want to sleep." Thursday or Friday is when they cover the lit biz. He promised to send me copies of everything when it came out. I had to promise him that I would call when I got back to Barcelona next week; maybe he could come with us to dinner, or to the airport at least. I was to contact him if I had any problems at all; the manager at Le Meridien had promised to get us a room in another nearby hotel if Le Meridien was completely booked up. We all promised to keep in touch by letter and fax. (In fact, I got a fax from Pablo three days after I was back in the U.S.) I thanked him again for everything—and swore a solemn oath that I would come back to Barcelona before too long.

I've become fixated on that thought over the years and haven't given up hope for a return visit yet, although the Barcelona I knew isn't the city I would see now.

*   *   *   *

We started toward the Museo Picasso on foot, and along the way, an older gentleman on La Rambla shouted "Pamela Sargent!" and then bowed to me. Maybe he had read the piece in *El País*.

I soon found that even a map wasn't much help in guiding us through the narrow maze of streets in the Old City. These are the kinds of streets you don't find in this country, old cobblestoned lanes that would be alleys over here but are still functioning streets there, with people out walking and the occasional car or motorbike whizzing by and scattering pedestrians. Finally we spied a cab, which got us to the Museo Picasso in two minutes. We might not have found the museum at all without the cab; it was down a really narrow old street. On the other hand, we might have, since tourists and tour groups were lined up outside.

The line moved quickly, and we were soon inside. We had wanted to come here because this museum has the largest number of works done in Picasso's early years, his formative period. We were curious to see what he had been up to before he found his own style. What we found was a lot of early work that was good, skilled stuff, much of it done in classical style and none of it even hinting at what was to come. Had Picasso kept going down that early road, he would have been a competent, well-trained, but unexceptional artist.

What we also found—and George really responded to these works—were some great drawings and etchings (this place has the largest collection of Picasso's drawings, too) that are both amusing and reveal something of the artist's personality. George was laughing to the point where some of the stuffier tourists in the vicinity were giving us funny looks. But what's the point, asked George later, of going to look at art in some stodgy state of mind and being stuffy and serious because you think culture is good for you? The artist would want you to *respond*. Picasso was a guy, I thought, after looking at many drawings with such titles as "The Artist, His Model, and Other Personages," who was probably often exasperated with all the people who would drop by his studio and distract him. There are sections devoted to all of his periods, which means you can see his development even if a lot of his most famous works are elsewhere. There is also a room devoted to Picasso's variations on Velázquez's "Las Meninas," in which you get the feeling that Picasso was taking Velázquez's painting apart and breaking it down into elements before synthesizing it into something else. He also managed in his deconstruction (at least it seemed so to me) to capture Velázquez's disdain for some of his subjects. Velázquez was a court painter who didn't much like some of the people he painted.

"I have a feeling," George said later, "that Picasso was the kind of guy you wouldn't be able to stand unless he thought you were his equal. Otherwise, he'd be unbearable." This was a man, after all, who refused to leave a will because he wanted his family and heirs to be fighting over his considerable fortune long after he was gone.

We had an iced tea in the courtyard of the museum, which was soon closing, and by then it was time to think about dinner.

We were looking for someplace inexpensive, since nobody else was going to pick up the tab this time. I had brought a couple of guides with me, my *Fodor's Spain* and *Barcelonawalks*, and leafed through the listings of inexpensive restaurants. Both guides, as it happened, recommended a place called Egipte, and we'd walked right by it; this restaurant was only about four blocks down La Rambla from our hotel. "There's a certain Henry Fieldingesque ambience about this brawling place," George Semler writes in Barcelonawalks. It sounded kind of rowdy, but what the hell? I figured that if two different guides had recommended Egipte, we couldn't go wrong.

We got there sometime after nine, meaning only a few customers were in the place, but it quickly filled up and was packed to the walls by close to midnight, which was when we left. Except for a few whores and a couple of leather boys who were downstairs in the bar having drinks, I didn't see anyone too disreputable. We came in from the street, went through the narrow bar area, and then had to climb a narrow flight of stairs to a balcony area that overlooks the bar and the street. It seemed a comfortable and cozy place, the kind of restaurant that draws "regulars," and if we'd come there any later, we might not have gotten a table. (There are some advantages to being from a country where people eat earlier; you can get to a restaurant before the crowds start coming.) The clientele seemed to be mostly Spanish couples and families, although there were a few German and Scandinavian tourists, too. The place was cheap, especially for Barcelona, the service was efficient, and the food was good. I tried an asparagus soufflé and a spicy beef dish with shrimp, while George had chicken with herbs and a huge green salad. We had a bottle of Cava with the meal, and even that didn't run up the bill much. The total cost came to something like 5500 pesetas, or about fifty bucks.

For my first three days in Barcelona, I had woken up every morning with intestinal pains. They always went away after about an hour or so, and I was never sure if it was the water (Barcelona's tastes terrible, and probably isn't any too good; I never saw anyone drinking any kind of water there except bottled water) or the weird mealtime hours. By now, though, I'd really gotten into eating late. In fact, it seemed a lot more sensible to dine until midnight and dawdle over my food than to eat earlier. Late eating hours also tend to provoke more interesting, heartfelt, and philosophical discussions; dinner was never boring in Spain.

We took our time wandering back to the hotel. The newsstands were still open; people of all ages were taking after-dinner walks. I did not want to leave. There would still be Sunday morning to wander around the city, since our plane didn't leave until the afternoon, but I felt this was the farewell point. I'd have to spend part of the morning packing and figuring out what we could leave behind at the hotel until we returned.

I bought some postcards. We went back to our room. I cried for a while before going to sleep. I *really* didn't want to leave.

SUNDAY, MAY 8, 1994

I spent part of the morning packing, part of it on the balcony, and part of it walking along La Rambla. The weather looked cloudy, which made me feel a little better about leaving. We ate breakfast late, and turned it into an early lunch by eating sandwiches made of rolls, meats, and cheeses, along with plenty of fruit, since there was a good chance we wouldn't eat again before nine that night.

The concierge stored the stuff we were leaving behind, so we wouldn't have to lug it all over Spain, and sent the porter and doorman out to get us a cab. (Five-star hotels don't let you do a thing for yourself.) We got to the Barcelona airport in less time than we had thought it might take. Once again, the airport was a model of cleanliness and efficiency. We checked in easily and boarded an Iberia jet that looked a lot newer and cleaner than the TWA rustbucket that had brought us to Spain.

A few passengers followed the custom of making the sign of the cross at boarding and later at takeoff. I leafed through the Iberia flight magazine, which had articles in Spanish and English. We were, according to the back of the magazine, entitled to one free drink on domestic flights, but had to pay for anything after that. No one under sixteen would be allowed to consume alcoholic beverages on the plane. That was how I found out that the drinking age in Spain is sixteen.

We were on our way to Santiago de Compostela, which lay at the other end of Spain, near the Atlantic. Santiago is famous largely for its humongous Gothic cathedral, which holds a central and important place in Spanish culture. Like many such cultural artifacts, its history is somewhat ambiguous.

According to my itinerary, Professor Cristina Blanco of the University of Santiago was to meet us at the airport and take us to our hotel, the Hostal San Francisco. I still wasn't sure whether Thomas Leary of the U.S. Embassy, who was to meet us in Santiago eventually, was going to be there later on or not. We couldn't see Santiago from the plane, since the town and the area around it were completely covered by clouds and fog. This, we found out, is normal weather for Santiago, where no one goes anywhere without an umbrella. The pilot made a couple of approaches before landing; I got the feeling he wanted to eyeball the runway and not just rely on his instruments to get him down. The landing was smooth; when we rolled to a stop, all the other passengers broke into applause.

We claimed our luggage and went out to the lobby. This airport wasn't much bigger than the one we had left in Binghamton. Santiago has only about a hundred thousand people, and the landscape, except for some palm trees, is a lot like Binghamton's. Professor Cristina Blanco somehow managed to spot us, and after we had walked out to the sidewalk near the parking lot so that her husband Cesar could get their car and come back for us, George and I were feeling very much at ease.

George summed it up later. "As soon as I saw them," he said, "I thought, great! They're people like us!" They were, in fact, a lot

---

THE CATHEDRAL OF SANTIAGO DE COMPOSTELA

In 813, it is said, a hermit was directed by a holy light to a field. He told people to start digging, and soon a sarcophagus said to contain the remains of St. James was uncovered. Nobody really knows how St. James's body allegedly got to Spain, since he was beheaded in Jerusalem not long after the crucifixion of Jesus Christ, but the body had been found at an opportune moment. The Muslim forces of the Moors had almost completely overrun Spain at that point. Some thirty years later, in 844, the Christian army won its first victory against the Muslims, and the soldiers claimed that St. James himself—Santiago as they called him—rode with them, armed with a huge sword and riding a big white horse. He became the patron saint of Spain, and Spanish fighting men used his name as a battle cry while ridding Spain of the Moors and also while slaughtering indigenous people in the Americas. People from all over Spain, and Catholics in other countries, too, often come to Santiago de Compostela on pilgrimages; in fact, there is a stone inside the cathedral placed there when Pope John Paul came to visit, designating the cathedral as a place of pilgrimage.

like the kinds of people I would expect to run into at our alma mater Binghamton University.

Cristina was a slim woman with long dark hair, big brown eyes, and the kind of long face you see in some Spanish paintings. Cesar was handsome, tall, and had curly hair; it turned out that he was a high school English teacher. Cristina was nervous at first. She had been pressed into service almost at the last minute, because Professor Constante Gonzalez, who had invited me and arranged to have me speak there, was in England. Professor Gonzalez had been hoping that he could change his plans, that the people in England who had him there annually for some sort of cultural exchange program would let him arrive there a few days later, but that proved to be impossible. He was so disappointed, she told me, upset and fearful that everything would go wrong. And Cristina had been saddled with looking after George and me only the day before, when Professor Gonzalez had regretfully boarded his flight to England.

"You won't like Santiago," Cristina said in mournful tones, "after Barcelona." And George and I replied, almost at the same time, "You're wrong. It's like home!" It was, too, as Cesar drove along the two-lane road that led to Santiago. It was raining, for one thing, and the climate was damp and made me feel arthritic. In other words, I even felt as though I was back home, except that Santiago is even damper than Binghamton.

Cesar told us a little about his students. "They don't like to work," he said. "They don't read enough, they watch too much television." The complaints sounded familiar. In fact, one of the problems in Spain, as it is in a lot of other parts of the world, is the influence of American popular culture. We've rotted our own minds, so now we can rot everyone else's, too.

The center of town was the oldest part of Santiago. We were right at the heart of the historic sites, only about a block away from the Gothic cathedral. The Hostal San Francisco turned out to be a monastery, part of which had been turned into a hotel for guests. Cristina looked relieved when we went into raptures over this place, because I think she was worried that we would find our quarters too modest. But the place was atmospheric, with a courtyard outside the lobby and the occasional monk wandering through the large sitting room. (It was a three-star hostelry, though, meaning that we had to schlepp our bags to our room ourselves, with help from Cristina and Cesar.) Our room, it was obvious, had once been a monk's cell, but the stone walls and high ceiling had been plastered and painted and the bathroom had all the usual amenities, including a bidet. Our two narrow twin beds turned out to be a lot more comfortable than they first appeared to be, and outside the windows, which were equipped with sturdy wooden shutters, was a view of mist-covered green hills. (I later discovered that Santiago's water tasted great; it was probably the best water I drank in Spain.)

It was about five o'clock. Cristina gave me her phone number and told me to call her when we were through sightseeing; she would take us out to dinner. We fortified ourselves with a couple of beers from the minibar (where the prices were a lot lower than in Barcelona) and some Motrin (a necessity for sightseeing in that damp cold climate), put on our raincoats, and headed outside with our umbrellas.

In this part of town, all the streets are cobblestoned. We headed down the narrow street that would lead us to the cathedral, and passed a cafe where somebody was listening to "Pump Up the Jam" at top volume—not the most appropriate piece of music in this medieval setting. We came to the wide cobblestoned expanse of the Plaza del Obradoiro, and got a good look at the historic cathedral.

This massive structure seemed almost to appear above us suddenly; it loomed over the plaza. The main entrance is two stories above the plaza; you have to climb a good number of stone steps to get inside. Two stairways zigzag down on either side; we made our way up a stairway to one of the doors and went inside.

We could glimpse the lighted altar in the distance—and it did seem awfully far away—so we had a long way to travel to get there. This cathedral is so huge that it was hard to estimate its size. It has to be smaller than St. Peter's Basilica, which had felt just as large to me when I visited it, but I'll bet it isn't that much smaller. We walked slowly around the cathedral, pausing every so often to rest on a bench along the sides. There were a few other tourists, and occasionally we would come upon somebody praying in one of the side chapels, but the place seemed almost empty. Once in a while, I looked up at the balconies and the Gothic arches curved high above them. This place was the goods, I thought, a real Christian shrine; you could feel the faith that had gone into building it even if you were an atheist.

In the back of the altar is a narrow staircase where you can climb up behind the huge statue of St. James and look down. We went up the stairs and found a priest sitting near the statue. A couple of people ahead of us followed custom and kissed the cloak, which is covered in jewels, of St. James, something George was not about to do. The priest smiled at us benevolently anyway; he was probably used to atheist and heretic tourists coming into the cathedral. The view from behind the statue of St. James was overwhelming; the whole area below was lighted, and there were draperies and sculptures of saints everywhere. This was all too much to take in all at once.

This cathedral may be a holy place, but commerce wasn't neglected. In a gift shop at one end of the cathedral, I bought a couple of postcards and George bought a huge chocolate with almonds bar with an etching of the cathedral on the wrapper. We were walking back toward the entrances when I noticed that more people seemed to be inside the church. The rows and rows of pews stretching out from the altar were filling up, and somebody was ringing a small bell every few minutes, so I suspected it was almost time for a mass.

My guess is that the cathedral could hold thousands. As we walked past the pews, it looked to me as though hundreds of people, maybe even more, had come into the place since we had arrived, and more were coming. Yet the size of the place was such that you still felt surrounded by space. At the confessionals, some people were making their confessions. These confessionals, to my eyes anyway, seemed odd. There were large carved wooden booths, and you could see the priests inside, sitting behind windows covered with screens, but anyone making a confession had to kneel outside the confessional on a kneeling board. "Isn't that kind of strange?" I whispered to George as a well-dressed blonde woman knelt outside one of the booths and crossed herself. "You don't have much privacy." He said, "I think the whole point is to be *seen* making your confession."

Almost all the seats were filled by then. We left and went outside to take a look at the Plaza. The Hotel de los Reyes Católicos is a huge palatial building on one side of this Plaza, and I found out later that it has been turned into a luxurious, but allegedly overpriced, hotel. It was originally built by King Ferdinand and Queen Isabella in the late

1400s. A man trying to sell records of traditional Galician folk music approached us and gave us his spiel, but we weren't buying.

Santiago is in Galicia. Just as the Catalan people in the part of Spain where Barcelona lies have Catalan (which is halfway to being French) as their native language, the Galicians speak Gallego, which is a mixture of Spanish and Portuguese. To complicate things even more, Galicians are descendants of the same Celts who settled the British Isles and Ireland long ago, which may account for the fact that bagpipes are a traditional instrument in this part of Spain.

We got back to the hotel at around eight, and I called Cristina. About half an hour later, she and Cesar came to pick us up for dinner. The evening inadvertently turned into a tour of the old part of Santiago, and maybe we should be grateful for that, because we got to see a lot of picturesque streets we otherwise might not have seen. The problem was that, because it was Sunday and Santiago is a small town, we couldn't find a restaurant that was open. Cesar would drive down one of the narrow winding streets (some were on steep hills, which didn't help) and park, and then we would head off toward an eatery only to find out it was closed. Eventually we drove toward the newer area of town. Some Roma kids were out panhandling and trying to get money for using squeegees on windshields, just the way street people did in New York; Cristina said that more gypsies had been coming into Spain lately, and that most of their kids didn't go to school, but instead became pickpockets and thieves. "But we don't really have much crime here," she said, "so you don't have to worry. It's not like Barcelona on La Rambla." Given that I had felt fairly safe in Barcelona, this was good to hear.

We didn't find any place to eat here, either. Cristina was getting visibly upset, so George and I reassured her that we had enjoyed the chance to see more of the town, while Cesar went across the street to make some phone calls to restaurants. I had noticed that, for a small town, the newer part of Santiago had a lot of heavy traffic and what looked like a lot of tall buildings. Cristina told me, as drizzle slowly seeped down from the sky, that here, as everywhere in Spain, people tended to crowd together. It's exactly the opposite of the U.S., where people tend to spread out. People in Spain like to be in the center of town, and the vast majority of them live in apartments. Cristina didn't think much of the construction, though. "Every once in a while," she told me, "a building falls down and people get killed. That's because the builders are incompetent and the inspectors are corrupt. They put up these buildings and don't care what happens later. They're not well-built at all!"

Cesar came back across the street. He had found a place that was open, a good restaurant where he had often gone himself. He went to get the car, and we were soon on our way to a place on the outskirts of town that looked, to my eyes anyway, reasonably classy. As for the food, I had heard that seafood was a specialty around here, and ordered a huge salad and then a main course that turned out to be fried fish stuffed with shrimp. It's misleading to describe it that way, because it was delicious.

Cristina and Cesar, we found out, had traveled to the U.S. as tourists not long before. They had seen New York City (which, believe it or not, they loved, despite being warned the whole time they were there to be careful), and had gone to San Francisco, where Cesar had come down with a fever and severe flu and Cristina had gone into a panic over his health. The only part of San Francisco he had ended up seeing was a hospital. "I hope you get a chance to go back," I said. "It really is a wonderful city." Cesar didn't look as though he believed me.

George asked Cristina if it was customary for people on planes to applaud upon landing safely. Apparently it was, almost everywhere in Spain. What about crossing yourself? "Oh, that's nothing," Cristina replied. "It's superstition, not religion—it's like knocking on wood. Religion's only on the surface here, it doesn't go deep." She discussed her own upbringing, which is apparently commonplace in Spain. "Everybody's baptized," she said. "You go to mass, you make your first communion." In her case, her parents had even sent her to a religious school, although they never went to church themselves. "When I was about eleven," Cristina went on, "I said, 'Why should I bother with all this if you don't?' And so they told me I didn't have to any more." This is a normal rite of passage, deciding not to bother with religion after a while, and Cristina claimed that most people under forty were totally uninterested in the church. "The church thinks everything's a sin anyway," Cristina said, "so why listen to it?" This widespread attitude makes Spain a profoundly Catholic country where a majority of the people aren't religious. George nodded, since he was brought up much the same way as Cristina. Needless to say, Cristina had her doubts about whether St. James's body was in fact buried in the local cathedral—and a lot of people are skeptical of that story.

(Still, Jacinto Antón of *El País* had told me during our interview that there was a growing interest in Spain in New Age stuff, shamanism, and Native American religions. So some people were looking for spiritual experiences elsewhere.)

We were working on our second bottle of wine by then. The scandals in the Spanish government came up; every day, it seemed, somebody else was resigning from office. Everyone was assuming that the former head of the National Guard had disappeared into some Central or South American refuge. George wondered if the government might fall. Both Cesar and Cristina said that there was no chance of that. However corrupt the Socialist government turned out to be, they were still preferable to the right wing. Everybody, Cristina said, was scared of the conservative forces; they were the kind of people who screamed imprecations at women going to abortion clinics (behavior Cristina found utterly loathsome). They also had links to Opus Dei, a secretive Catholic organization so far to the right that the Pope was a flaming radical by comparison. "The conservative leader looks just like Hitler!" she exclaimed. People in Spain, Cesar said, were sick of blood and fighting. They had seen too much of it during the Civil War, they had gone through their troubles with terrorists, and everyone remembered that the government had nearly been overthrown by a military coup as recently as 1981. (Only the king had prevented it by summoning military leaders loyal to him from around the country.) So no one really thought that the government was in any danger now.

This led to a discussion of politicians in general. Paula Jones and her accusations against President Clinton were in the news by then. Why did Americans care about such things, anyway? It was widely known in Spain that various ministers in the government had mistresses and children out of wedlock, and that King Juan Carlos messed around, and nobody cared. "Nobody here runs for office talking about family values," Cristina said. That only happens in the U.S. and England, which had recently followed our example. It seemed, to her mind, a recipe for hypocrisy.

George was worrying that maybe we were keeping our hosts up too late. Cristina and Cesar laughed off that concern. "Usually," Cristina told us, "I don't even start thinking about supper until eleven-thirty, maybe later—and then I have all these nightmares!" These nightmares are also an accepted part of life, since we heard approximately the same thing in other places. You eat late, and often spend a good part of the night drinking, and then you go to bed and have nightmares. Or you just stay up and drink until dawn and then sleep a few hours. It's only natural to have nightmares! It never occurs to anybody that maybe eating supper a little earlier might help.

Cristina and Cesar also talked about their honeymoon, which is a story in itself. They had married in the mid-1980s and in a fit of idealism had decided to go to Cuba, being under the illusion that it was a progressive society. It was also a return to her roots of sorts for Cristina, since one of her grandmothers had grown up in Havana before moving to Spain. They were horrified at what they found. Stores that only took hard currency and which Cubans weren't allowed to enter, stores exactly like the Berioskas I had seen when traveling in the former Soviet Union on the eve of its collapse. People terrified of talking to anyone, since just about every block had a busybody who would report any subversive-sounding gab to the authorities. Buildings in disrepair, beaches fenced off for tourists, prostitutes around the tourist hotels. People routinely had stuff stolen from their luggage on the way out of Cuba, too, if they didn't take the precaution of bribing the customs officials. Cristina recalled one telling incident when she and Cesar were leaving. A team of Cuban athletes were going through customs, on their way to some tournament. One of the athletes made the mistake of laughing—didn't say anything, just laughed. He was dragged away by security and held for some hours, presumably so that they could find out exactly why he had laughed. They finally let him go, but he didn't look as though he would be laughing again any time soon. The trip had been extremely disillusioning, and Cristina had told her grandmother after returning, "Don't go back. It isn't what you remember."

We had gotten to the restaurant sometime after nine-thirty. It was after midnight when we left. By then, we were all in a fairly jolly mood. We said goodbye to Cesar, and promised to write (we weren't going to see him the next day, since he had to teach).

Back at the hotel (or monastery), the concierge handed me a handwritten note. It was from Thomas Leary, the cultural attaché from the U.S. Embassy, who had arrived there from Madrid at about ten-thirty. "Call me when you get in," the note said, and noted his room number, but by then it was close to one in the morning. So I left a note of my own with the concierge, telling Thomas Leary that we had gotten back late and that he could call my room in the morning, or meet us for breakfast. Maybe he was used to Spanish hours, but I had my doubts about the wisdom of calling a fellow American at one A.M.

MONDAY, MAY 9, 1994

I was getting dressed when Tom Leary called the room. It was around eight-thirty or nine; he had already eaten breakfast, but might join us for coffee.

We packed and went down to the dining room. No bounteous repast here; it was coffee and croissant time, with some juice and fruit on the side. Still, after eating fairly late, we weren't hungry.

Then Tom Leary showed up. He was a tall, lanky guy in his late thirties, with glasses and dark hair, almost nerdy-looking in appearance. He was wearing a dark suit, white shirt, and tie, and carrying a briefcase. He looked as though he could be working for the C.I.A. on some covert operation. All of which shows how misleading first impressions can be, because Tom, as we were to find out, was a lot cooler and more like us in his attitudes and opinions than we realized.

We introduced ourselves, and had more coffee. Tom was also worried about Professor Gonzalez's absence, but I assured him that we'd been well looked after. Professor Gonzalez, he told me, was a great guy, and apparently legendary for his sense of humor; he would be extremely disappointed at having to miss me. Tom would come to my lecture, and to lunch afterward, and then we would all fly to Madrid together. And he didn't mind coming up to Santiago on my behalf, since he appreciated being able to get out of Madrid and see other parts of the country.

We went through the business of checking out and arranging for the hotel to store our luggage, and then Professor Patricia Fra, a small, red-haired woman with greenish eyes and a British accent, came by to drive us to the university. Cristina, as it happened, couldn't pick us up, since Cesar needed the car to drive to work. We didn't have far to go to get to the University, which seems to inhabit much of the town. The medical school is in the old city, but most of the other departments are housed in new buildings that don't look unlike some recent State University of New York construction; they're glassy, low, red-brick or gray-brick buildings.

Several of the buildings bore graffiti. We saw quite a lot of graffiti in Spain, although usually it was only in certain places, among them university campuses, bridges, certain walls, and the sides of buildings overlooking railroad tracks. Some of it was the same sort of colorful, spray-painted graffiti you could have seen in New York or Los Angeles. In Spain, most of it was political graffiti. Here, at the University of Santiago, it was anti-draft graffiti, since male citizens of Spain still have to do military service. It was also anti-Spanish graffiti, much of it written in Gallego and not Spanish. The general sentiment seemed to be, "Spain, get out of Galicia!"

"It's definitely a change," Tom Leary said. "Not long ago, most of it was anti-American graffiti." That didn't surprise me, either. After all, the U.S. had supported Franco's regime.

We went to Patricia's office, and ran into Cristina, whose office was just down the hall. There I was introduced to Professor Manuel Miguez, a gray-haired professorial-looking man, who was to introduce me at my talk. But before I did anything else, a television reporter was waiting with her crew, wanting an interview with me. We went down to the room where I was to give my speech (this room looked like the usual large college classroom on a State University of New York campus), to meet the reporter, who was a gorgeous, raven-haired woman in a black miniskirt. She wanted to ask me lots of questions about women's writing, and women in science fiction, so I sat near the front of the room, with Patricia next to me to interpret, while the reporter grilled me and her cameraman taped me. Towards the end, thinking of Pablo, I managed to get in some comments about my Genghis Khan novel. The television reporter was interested in women's issues, and the novel's largely written from the points-of-view of women, so it was definitely relevant to the discussion.

The speech, scheduled for 12:30, began closer to one. By the time Professor Miguez was introducing me, I was starting to get more nervous. Now I was going to have to prove myself to Tom Leary, who had set up this part of the trip. I didn't want him thinking that the U.S. Information Service had wasted its time and money. The talk I gave was "Science Fiction, Historical Fiction, and Alternative History," the same one I had delivered at the University of Barcelona, although I varied my extraneous comments here. Again, in spite of warnings that the audience would be shy, I not only had questions, but three members of the audience came up to talk to me afterward at length.

One was a young woman who had asked, from the audience, "Are there any new novels about biological developments?" (I was to hear this question again in Madrid, and my answer was that there weren't. Why? I think it's because most writers have no idea where we're headed now; so much is being learned that even scientists who are specialists in certain areas can't keep up with them.) The other two were young men, in normal college student garb of jeans, T-shirts, and jackets, and what struck me about all of them was that they were so much like people I had met at science fiction gatherings over here; they had the same intensity—some might call it obsessiveness. They were all fairly familiar with the literature, but were necessarily limited to what was available in Spain, so there were gaps in what they had read; some writers who are among the most important here were completely unknown to them. They also felt isolated (this was true of such sf readers in the U.S. back then, although science fiction is much more culturally dominant these days); it wasn't often that they met people who shared their interest. But they had even more reason for feeling isolated, since the audience for science fiction in Spain was smaller than it was here.

At last Patricia and Cristina had to intervene, so that there would be time for lunch before we had to go to the airport. I had to promise to send them copies of the speech, since they knew that the absent Professor Gonzalez would want to read it. Tom was happy with the speech, too, since I had covered a lot of territory and done something that, to him anyway, seemed original. One of my worries had been setting a context for anyone who might not be familiar with some of the things I was talking about, while making the talks interesting and enlightening for those who knew more. I knew that I couldn't assume that most of my references would be familiar (as I might with an American audience), but couldn't talk down to people, either.

The weather, miraculously for Santiago, was clearing up; we could even see a bit of sunshine. As we walked over to the faculty dining area, Patricia told me about one of her problems when she was in the U.S. She had been at Brown one summer, doing research, and had found it almost impossible to get used to the air-conditioning. "When I went to the library," she said, "it was like walking into a freezer! I would go to stores and see people working in heavy sweaters!" She couldn't understand why so many of us required such low temperatures. This was something I couldn't really explain, being somebody with a very low tolerance for heat myself.

The faculty dining room turned out to be a restaurant with waiters, white tablecloths, linen napkins, and crystal goblets. We ate on a closed-in balcony area overlooking a small green park, fountain, and artificial lake where some ducks and geese were waddling about with their young. By then, the sun had come out. We had two traditional dishes for that area, one a large dish of green beans cooked in olive oil, and the other a meat stew with little potatoes.

We talked about a lot of things, including books and movies; Patricia was doing a dissertation on certain important American novels that had been made into movies, among them *The Great Gatsby* and *The Old Man and the Sea*. Her contention was that filmmakers should try to use cinematic conventions, rather than literary ones, in their movies, that trying to be too true to the book and making what amounted to an illustrated version was an artistic mistake. Another subject we discussed was the prevalence of lawsuits in the U.S. This kind of litigiousness doesn't exist in Spain, or many other places, as far as I can tell. No matter what you do, I said, it's gotten to the point where you have to consider how liable you might be, and often feel is if you shouldn't leave your home without a lawyer. Tom allowed as how he had never been involved in a lawsuit, not even peripherally, and I said he might be one of the few Americans who hasn't. Maybe it's because he's lived outside the country for almost his whole adult life.

The subject of therapy came up. The general consensus at the table was that a lot of what passes for psychotherapy is akin to superstitious practices, or a racket. I found it interesting that even two women who are very familiar with American culture, who have mastered the language and traveled in our country, whose specialty is American language and literature, find our penchant for lawsuits, psychotherapy, and self-help groups mysterious and exotic.

At last we had to leave for the hotel and then the airport, and here again I was sorry we couldn't stay longer. By now, the day had turned sunny, which made me even more regretful about leaving. We said our farewells to Cristina on the campus and to Patricia at the airport, and added more addresses to the pile of cards I was accumulating.

At this point, I should mention that the custom in Spain, when greeting or saying goodbye to somebody, is to hold the person gently by the arms and administer a kiss on each cheek. People who are friends may be hugged, too.

On the plane, another tidy new Iberia jet, Tom gave me a copy of the announcement for my speech at the Casa de America in Madrid. Eduardo Garrigues, the Director-General of the Casa de America (and who also has a position in the Spanish government; he used to run Spain's consulate in Los Angeles, I was told) had *asked* to introduce me, being a fan of mine. This was unheard of, according to Tom; usually people had to beg him just to show up. We settled back for the flight.

* * * *

I had picked up a little knowledge about Madrid, but not much, and didn't know what to expect. "Madrid's a capital city," John Zvereff had said, implying that Barcelona had more going for it. Still, Madrid also had a reputation for being pretty lively, even if it was more formal than Barcelona. I also knew that people there ate even later than in other parts of Spain, but at least now our digestive systems were prepared for that.

We hadn't been able to see much of Madrid from the air on the TWA flight. This time, I had a clear view. Madrid sits on top of a large plateau; you see these rocky, sometimes reddish-looking cliffs on the side of the plateau, and eventually, after flying over land that's considerably more dry and barren-looking than the green hills around Santiago, you spot Madrid. The airport looks imposing from the plane, with long buildings that look as though they might house a military complex, but the terminal we passed through was fairly modern. It wasn't efficient, though; we and the other passengers were wandering down one hallway and up another before we finally found the carousel where our bags could be claimed, and even then Tom had to talk a maintenance man into opening the door so that we could go inside.

Taxis were lined up outside the airport; we took one to our hotel, a glassy tower called the Hotel Castellana Intercontinental. It sat near a large traffic circle (with the U.S. Embassy practically around the corner) on one of Madrid's main thoroughfares, the Paseo de Castellana. This was, in other words, another centrally located place that would make it easier for us to get around. Drivers in Madrid, I noticed on the way to the hotel, liked to step on the gas; they speeded noticeably more than Barcelona drivers, who weren't exactly slow. There was also one hell of a lot of traffic; we had arrived in time for the evening rush hour. I had the impression as we sped along on the highway that there were a lot of new, modern, glassy, skyscraper sorts of buildings.

Tom assured us that our quarters here would be the equal of Le Meridien's. Our room turned out to be another humongous suite, with a sitting area, a huge bed, lots of closet space, and even a small dressing room next to the bathroom, which had two large sinks. In fact, the Hotel Castellana was a four-star hotel, not a five-star job (by now, we were capable of drawing such fine distinctions); the furniture in the room looked worn, there wasn't much of a view, you had to wait longer to get an elevator and share it with people (Le Meridien had a way of automatically controlling its elevators so that you never shared yours with anyone else unless they happened to be waiting with you on the same floor at exactly the same time), and, as we found out later, there weren't going to be any chocolate treats and bottled water by the bed. But the lobby contained a large and comfortable area where people could sit, order drinks, read newspapers, even log on (there were a few computer terminals scattered around the room), and the staff was extremely helpful. I'd definitely recommend the place.

Tom had to head off to the embassy after getting us checked in. He called later to tell us that a Carlos Aganzo of a newspaper called *Ya* wanted to interview me, and that I was to meet him in the hotel lobby at ten in the morning; an interpreter from the embassy would join us. So, until I delivered my speech at seven in the evening, we would have most of the day to explore Madrid. We had already decided what the main order of business would be—going to the Museo del Prado, which was only a short cab ride away.

In the meantime, we could check out Madrid this evening, which we did, discovering that people are out roaming around and sitting in outdoor bars and cafes at all hours, much as they do in Barcelona, except that the people of Madrid seem to spend even more time out on their streets. We weren't all that hungry, though, after our large lunch, so eventually we went back to the hotel, where we discovered that we could sit in a beautiful patio area with trees just outside the lobby, and have a waiter bring us a light meal and wine. We went to bed early by Spanish standards, at around twelve-thirty.

TUESDAY, MAY 10, 1994

When I telephoned the U.S. Embassy in Madrid, I had to go through their voice mail system. A voice in English and then Spanish told me to say "one" if I had an emergency or needed to report a stolen passport or "two" if I needed to contact one of the departments there. Then I had to let it know if I wanted to speak in English or Spanish. After that there's more rigmarole until you finally get the phone of the person or department you want ringing, and nine times out of ten nobody answers anyway. It's almost faster to leave the hotel, walk down the street, and then head around the corner to the embassy to settle your problem in person.

I was to find out about the embassy's voice mail system later, but first I had to stoke myself with some breakfast and get ready for the interview with Carlos Aganzo. The hotel restaurant was in a large, comfortable room down a flight of stairs from the lobby, with long couches against the walls and chairs with arms around most of the tables. The breakfast was up to Le Meridien's standards; you could find just about anything at the buffet table, including Jabon ham if you wanted any at that hour. Every once in a while, a waiter would come around with coffee and milk. I was eating by myself, since George had decided to sleep a little longer, and then I discovered that the teenaged girl sitting to my right with her mother and her mother's good-looking male friend was a fellow American. I knew it as soon as the young woman opened her mouth to say, "I was like, 'Yeah, I'm really glad to be *here*?' (rising inflection) and Mom was like, 'I knew you'd love *Madrid*?'" I also knew that the people on my right were French, not just because they were speaking that language, but also because they were complaining about the food.

It occurs to me that I haven't yet said anything about tipping in Spain. It was an extremely simple system, because the Spaniards just added the tip (about fifteen per cent) to most of the bills they gave you. It was all right to leave some small change on the table for waiters who have given good service, to give cab drivers extra change by rounding up, to give porters small amounts for carrying bags or doing something extra, and slip the doorman fifty pesetas (about 40 cents) for getting you a cab, but generally people in Spain seemed too proud to worry about tips.

I was in the lobby's sitting area at a little before ten. Someone had left an *International Herald Tribune* behind, so I was in the middle of reading that when a small, slim middle-aged woman with long curly black hair came over to me and introduced herself as Blanca Novo, my interpreter from the embassy's Press Section. "I thought it was you," she told me. "You're the only person here who looks as bewildered as I do!" In fact, Blanca was extremely annoyed with Carlos Aganzo for being so late; by then, it was almost 10:20.

"Maybe he's stuck in traffic," I said. It was all right with me if we waited a while longer. Blanca told me that Mr. Aganzo was in charge of *Ya*'s large back page, where he could interview anyone he liked, and that it was a good place to have an interview. My publisher would be pleased, especially since journalists in Madrid could be touchy when somebody had already gotten a lot of coverage in Barcelona, and often decided to ignore them in a fit of pique. (Somebody has described the rivalry between Madrid and Barcelona as akin to a blood feud.) We chatted for a while, and by 10:40, Blanca was really pissed off. This was unforgivable! She would have words with Carlos Aganzo! She told me to call her at the embassy if I heard anything from him, and gave me her extension number. Off she went, and I went back upstairs.

I had put on a dress for the interview, but changed into slacks and a big shirt for the Prado. George had eaten breakfast by then, and we were on our way out of the room when the phone rang. Carlos Aganzo was calling. George spoke to him, given that Mr. Aganzo's English was rudimentary, and managed to find out 1) that this reporter had thought the interview was scheduled for eleven, and 2) that some looming domestic crisis was demanding his attention, so he couldn't wait any longer. George told him to hang on if he could for a few minutes, and then I called the embassy, threading my way through the voice mail maze and finally leaving a message with one of Blanca's colleagues. There was no point in going downstairs; without my interpreter, there could be no interview anyway. So off Carlos Aganzo went, after calling the room one last time. By then, George was convinced, perhaps unfairly, that Carlos Aganzo was a flake and that he'd been drinking. We were on our way out of the room again when Blanca called back. She was absolutely furious with the man from *Ya*; it had been very clear that the interview was to be at ten. In fact, she had talked him out of coming over any earlier, so that I wouldn't have to get up too early. (Given Blanca's own punctuality, and the fact that Tom Leary had praised her for her reliability and skill in handling the press, I believed her.) She could probably get him to interview me tomorrow, but I had put myself out quite enough for him! Well, I wasn't thinking of the reporter, but of Pablo Somarriba and my responsibility to my publisher. I told Blanca that, if *Ya* wanted an interview the next day, and there was time to schedule it, I would do one.

Something had finally gone wrong on this trip, but at least it was something relatively minor.

* * * *

The Prado was only a five-minute ride by cab down the Paseo de Castellana. I had figured that, given our limited time, this was the Madrid museum to check out. If there had been more time, we would have gone to the Centro de Arte Reina Sofia, a new modern museum with Picassos, Mirós, and other works, but we didn't have time, which means we now have still another excuse to go back to Spain in the future.

You enter the museum by climbing up steep flights of stairs to the second floor main entrance, or go in at the ground floor entrance. You're advised to go in the main entrance, so naturally we entered

---

ABOUT THE PRADO

The Museo del Prado is one of the great art museums of the world, on a par with the Louvre, the Uffizi, the Hermitage, and the Metropolitan Museum of Art. The building, completed in 1819, has the world's largest collections of the works of Spain's great artists Francisco Goya, Diego Velázquez, and El Greco. Because Spain once ruled an empire, there are also many Flemish and Italian paintings in the Prado, including works by Rubens, Rembrandt, Titian, and Botticelli.

through the ground floor entrance instead, avoiding the stairs. In this section, you find Goya's drawings and also paintings from his "Black Period," the ones he did near the end of his life. These paintings are stunning, but also bloody, disturbing (one of the most famous is "Saturn Devouring One of His Sons," which gives you an idea), and depressing, so maybe it was just as well that we saw them first before viewing Goya's earlier works upstairs. This was a guy who had nightmares! We spent about an hour there before heading upstairs, where I bought a guide, a necessity for wandering through a museum of this size, because otherwise you'd never find the particular things you want to see.

We gorged ourselves on El Grecos, Velázquezes (including "Las Meninas," the painting Picasso deconstructed, and various paintings of mythological scenes; Velásquez was one of the few Spanish painters to paint scenes drawn from myth), and earlier Goyas, including the famous "Nude Maja" and "Clothed Maja." The story is (and it may be apocryphal) that Goya was commissioned to paint this woman by her husband, fell in love with her, painted her in the nude, and then had to do another painting of her quickly with her clothes on to hide the affair from the husband. We also viewed a number of works by Rubens (anybody who is overweight will feel slimmer after gazing at his nudes) and Bosch's celebrated "Garden of Earthly Delights." In the same room is Bosch's "Table of the Seven Deadly Sins," which shows scenes from the Dutch life of his time, and which caused an American tourist near us to announce, "The deadliest sin is not paying off your second mortgage!" We saw a lot at the Prado, and got to spend time studying the works, but as with any great museum, we would probably need months to explore it thoroughly. And anyone going to a museum every day wouldn't need an exercise program, with all the walking and the staircases.

We ate lunch in the Prado's cafeteria at around four (and our salads weren't bad, either), looked at some more paintings afterward, and then decided reluctantly to leave. I had to give a speech at seven.

* * * *

The Casa de America, where I was to speak, is housed in a palace, the Palacio de Linares. This palace, which wasn't renovated until 1992, is supposed to be haunted, and there are people who claim to have seen or sensed a ghost there. The ghost is supposedly that of a child who was born of an incestuous relationship and then killed to keep that affair secret. That's one version of the story, anyway; there are several, but they all involve incest and a dead child.

Tom Leary came to the hotel to pick us up. With him was another embassy employee, Macarena Moreno, who, as it happened, was a science fiction fan. ("Our resident expert," Tom called her.) She had recently acquired a copy of *Asimov y sus amigos* and was looking forward to reading my story "Strip-Runner." (The title in Spanish is "La corredora de cintas.") We didn't have far to go to the Casa de America, which we had passed on the way to the Prado, but a disappointment was in store. Eduardo Garrigues, the government minister who had been dying to introduce me, wasn't going to be there, and the government's ongoing crisis and scandals seemed to be the reason for his absence. By then, it almost sounded as though the government was in meltdown, but the prime minister had announced he wasn't going to resign, and that announcement, despite the scandal surrounding him, seemed to relieve everybody. (I never did get to meet Mr. Garrigues, but when I got home, I had a fax from Tom Leary ordering some of my books and asking how much they would cost. He specifically requested that one set be autographed and inscribed to Eduardo Garrigues. So I could hope that maybe he would be so disappointed at missing me that he would invite me back to Spain.)

On the other hand, the tardy and confused Carlos Aganzo of *Ya* was going to interview me after all. He had apologized profusely to Blanca Novo, and a new appointment had been set up for the next day.

Talk about great settings for giving a speech! The room at the Casa de America set aside for me was gorgeous, with gold leaf trimming and a *trompe d'oeil* painting on the ceiling that made it seem as though you were gazing up at the sky, while cherubs and such apparitions were peering down at you over a railing. In the middle of this painting were two beautiful women in diaphanous robes, just floating there. (The original owner of the palace was definitely a connoisseur of beautiful babes, because some nude ones had been painted on the ceiling of one of the bedrooms.) The crowd coming in and sitting down in the rows of chairs included three of Tom's colleagues from the cultural section of the embassy, all of them men in conservative dark suits and white shirts.

(By this time, I had picked up a few tidbits about previous writer-guests. Tom, being a diplomat, was discreet and would certainly not tell any scandalous or insulting stories, but he did mention having to search all over the hotel for William Kennedy, finally locating him in the bar. "Well," I said, "it's a safe bet that if you're going to meet a writer somewhere, and can't find him, always look in the bar!" The poet Allen Ginsburg, before his arrival, had told people that he was on a macrobiotic and vegetarian diet. This was obviously going to be a problem in Spain, but apparently the embassy had put together a list of places where he could eat. Then, as Tom put it, Allen Ginsburg got there and decided not to keep to his diet during his visit, which indicates to me that Ginsburg is sane. Questions I was frequently asked by the embassy's Spanish employees were, "Are you on a special diet? Are there foods you can't eat? Do you have to abstain from alcohol?" Did they ever look relieved when I admitted that I would eat almost anything and enjoyed my wine. People seem to expect Americans now to be fussy about food, on low-fat or vegetarian diets, bothered by cigarette smoke, and to complain about late meal hours, too; we have become the whiners of the world.)

I was introduced to Carmen Flys, one of the people associated with the Casa de America and a pretty young woman with black hair and what can only be called flashing brown eyes, to Juan Nuñez, a professor who was to be one of my hosts at the Complutense University of Madrid the next morning, and then it was time to give my talk on "The Role of Women in Science Fiction."

I assume this talk didn't lay an egg, mainly because people told me afterward that they had enjoyed it and also because, once again, I was asked a lot of questions by the audience. Carmen Flys and Macarena Moreno seemed especially taken by the subject, and Juan Nuñez got in a few queries, and then one of the embassy guys asked me the question all writers wince at, which is, "Where do you get your ideas?" This is a lot like asking, "How do you breathe?" So I had to explain to him (as I have millions of times before, and undoubtedly will again) that ideas are all over the place and that having them isn't the problem; it's figuring out what to do with them and which ones are worth writing about.

Tom had promised me that we would get a tour of the Palacio de Linares, that Carmen would show me around. This would take some doing, because it was against regulations and the old maintenance man on duty had a habit of forbidding access to anyone and calling the police if he found people wandering about. (He was a civil service employee, I found out later, dating from the days of Franco, and the Casa de America people were stuck with him because he couldn't be fired.) So we collected at the door, and then somehow I found myself on an elevator with Carmen, Juan Nuñez, a tall good-looking male journalist with a microphone and tape recorder who wanted to do a radio interview with me, and a gray-bearded professor of economics who had been in the audience and had some sort of association with the Casa de America. Off we were carried to the upper floors, but I figured everybody else would catch up with us sooner or later.

At this point, Juan Nuñez, an athletic-looking man with large gray eyes and the air of somebody about to go off the deep end, cornered me in the elevator. ("Cornered" is an accurate description, since Spaniards tend to stand at closer proximity than Americans do when they're talking to you.) He told me that my speech was wonderful, that he had found it fascinating, but—would it be possible to do something less formal for his class, something more about the process of writing and my own experiences and development as a writer, something more from the heart, so to speak? Holy shit, I thought to myself, he wants me to do an extemporaneous speech, without notes—something I had never done in my life, and a task I had always believed beyond my capacities.

What could I say? I stood there, my insides churning, as I calmly replied that of course I could do a talk like that instead. How the hell to accomplish that was something I didn't dare think about. Anyway, that was tomorrow; I would try to put it out of my mind that evening.

We left the elevator and Carmen showed us several of the palace's rooms. The chapel had paintings with religious themes, the bedroom a painting of nude babes, and the ballroom—this was where I began to understand where the story about ghosts had come from. We were standing just inside the doorway, looking at the darkened ballroom, when I felt a chill. There was a cold spot in the room, almost as if *an unseen entity* was standing there and pressing against me with its icy body. Why was that spot so cold? This was Madrid, in May, where the daytime temperature was near 80 degrees Fahrenheit (it had been 90 degrees the week before we arrived), and the palace wasn't air conditioned.

We didn't linger long, and followed Carmen down a long staircase that looked like a scaled-down version of the one in the Winter Palace in St. Petersburg. The cobblestones outside the doorway below, Carmen explained, weren't made of stone, but of wood. The mistress of the house had complained about the noise of horses and carriages on stones. So her husband had torn up all the stones and replaced them with wood.

It was a beautiful palace, and so recently restored that no one had yet done a book of photographs or a guide to the place. This prospect intrigued the radio reporter, who began speculating out loud about doing such a guide himself. In the meantime, it was becoming all too obvious that, for some reason, there was bad blood between Juan Nuñez and the professor of economics. The economist would mutter under his breath whenever Professor Nuñez was out of earshot, calling him "that impossible man" and something in Spanish that sounded much worse, and Dr. Nuñez in his turn would show his disdain for the economist by glaring at him in silence or snarling something to Carmen.

When we finally got back to the room where I had lectured, everyone else had disappeared. The economist wasn't worried about that; we could sit outside at one of the tables on the patio until everybody else showed up. So we went out to the patio. We sat around for a while in the clear dry beautiful air of a Madrid evening. The radio reporter was still trying to get an interview with me, and apparently willing to wait as long as necessary for it. Carmen eventually went off with Juan Nuñez to check out the palace, in case the people we had lost were about to emerge, and the economist wandered away (perhaps also hoping to put some distance between himself and Professor Nuñez), and I was alone with the reporter.

At last he could get his interview! The traffic was streaming by on the street next to the palace, but the sounds were muted, a dim hum in the background. A gentle breeze had picked up. The reporter wanted to ask me questions about women in science fiction and about my Genghis Khan book. I can't remember most of the questions, but we were having a fine time talking until the economist, Carmen, and Juan Nuñez reappeared. The reporter packed up his equipment and said his farewells—he had to get back to the radio studio—and George, Tom Leary, and everybody else had still not shown up. Apparently they weren't anywhere to be found inside the palace, either.

The economist wasn't worried. He started talking about how, when William Kennedy had been there some months before, people had wandered off in different directions and eventually touched base in one of the local sidewalk bars; presumably, we could do the same. So off we wandered.

It must have been about nine by then, but people were all over the place, strolling along the streets, catching buses, hailing cabs. We were walking along the same main thoroughfare that was a continuation of the Paseo de Castellana, the avenue that ran from our hotel down to the Prado. In the middle of the street, separating the two lanes of speeding traffic, was a huge space of trees, grass, cafes, and bars that was much too broad to be called a safety island; it was more like a long, thin park. We crossed the street and were soon ambling past a long row of gigantic sculptures that I will always remember as "the big fat statues." Because that was basically what they were, huge monumental black stone sculptures of big fat naked people (one that particularly struck my fancy was of a huge woman lying on her stomach with her big butt sticking up), nude men and women in various poses. These statues had become so popular in Madrid that traffic had been rerouted and a new road built so that people could cross the street to look at them more easily.

The economist urged us on, saying that it was about time we settled down at one of the local bars and started drinking. There was no reason to worry. I was only wandering around with total strangers in a foreign city of three million people, and eventually Tom Leary, who was surely experienced in finding lost writers, would catch up with me.

Carmen finally found the bar she had been looking for, and we scoped out the nearby outdoor tables, looking for a place to sit down. Yes, she assured me, they had wandered to exactly this same spot with William Kennedy, and in the fullness of time, the other people in the party made their way there. The tables were packed, and several of the people seated there were couples with young children or babies; this was, after all, about nine o'clock on a weekday evening in Madrid, which meant everybody was out walking, socializing, breathing the pleasant dry evening air, drinking wine, and thinking about where they would eat dinner later.

Just as a table emptied out, and we got ready to claim it, I spied George's Panama hat and the lanky form of Tom Leary coming toward us past the trees lining the highway. Everything was cool! They had figured on finding us somewhere around there.

Tom guided a small, round-faced woman with short dark hair toward me and introduced her as "Rachel Norniella, who also works at the embassy." We shook hands, and Rachel took the chair next to me. I was really slow that night, because it took a few minutes before it finally dawned on me that Rachel Norniella was Tom's wife. (Tom later told me that Rachel definitely "does not like being addressed as Mrs. Leary," and I was happy to learn that the Foreign Service, once an outpost of conventional and traditional behavior, doesn't mind if married women keep their own names and their jobs.) We all settled down for tapas and drinks; Tom had told us earlier that we would be going to dinner with him later. (I will mention in passing that the olives served there may qualify as the best in Spain, if not the world.)

There was some humorous banter about Barcelona and Catalunyan politics when I mentioned how delightful Barcelona had been. Tom told a story of a recent letter that had been sent to the embassy from the mayor of Barcelona. The letterhead had said, "Barcelona, España (Spain)," and everyone had been amazed that it hadn't simply spelled out, "Barcelona, Catalunya." This led to talk about the still-notorious ads Barcelona had done to publicize the 1992 Olympics. The ads, published in magazines and newspapers all over the world (I remembered seeing them in the *New York Times* and *Newsweek*), had begun with a line something like "Come to a land where the people always smile and the sun always shines, a beautiful country known as"—turn the page—"CATALUNYA," in big bold letters. The Spanish government officials in Madrid had gone into fits of rage over those ads. Tom then mentioned, and this came as a surprise to at least a couple of people, including me, that the official first language of instruction in Catalunya's schools was now Catalan, not Spanish; everybody would of course learn Spanish, as they always had, but it would not be the most important language in the schools. Math, science, history, whatever would all be taught in Catalan. "They're not even cutting foreigners as much slack," Tom went on. "Now they expect them to pick up more Catalan, too." I could understand the motive for this, but it still struck me as short-sighted, given that so many people speak Spanish and only about six million speak Catalan.

Juan Nuñez had to make his departure; as he clasped my hands, I assured him again that I would give a wonderful talk to his students. The economist, Macarena, and an embassy guy eventually said their farewells, too.

Here, I should mention that greeting people in Spain, or saying goodbye, generally required that you get up off your duff and stand. You can't just sit there, lolling around in your chair. If people are stopping by and leaving at different times, this may require you to do quite a bit of popping up and down at frequent intervals.

George and I had assumed that Carmen Flys was a Spanish citizen; in fact, she was from the U.S., another American expatriate like John Zvereff who was more at home in Spain. She was Ukrainian on her father's side and Spanish on her mother's; since her mother was Roman Catholic and her father adhered to the Church's Byzantine Rite, she had gone through two First Communions as a child and divided her time between two different churches. "Every time I went," she said, "I had to keep remembering which way to cross myself!" She knew Ukrainian, Spanish, and English, but definitely considered Spanish the only language in which to make love, a preference she mentioned while casting significant glances at George.

She also told us about the Casa de America's activities, which include English language classes, cultural exchanges, and courses for a Master's Degree in American Studies. Interestingly, a Master's in American Studies is, according to Carmen, almost completely useless in any practical sense. "The students," she said, "study just because they're interested." Some concentrated on American literature, others on American law or history or politics, but it was largely for themselves. On top of that, there was no such thing as a recognized master's degree in Spain, so it wasn't even something that could be put on a resumé there. Students earned a bachelor's degree; if they went on to graduate study, they got a doctorate or no degree at all. On top of that, there was almost no financial support for college-level academic work in Spain, no system of loans, scholarships, fellowships, grants-in-aid, or any other financial incentives. On the graduate level, people worked at other full-time jobs to support their studies; almost no one was a full-time student. On the undergraduate level, it was normal for students to still be living with their families. I mentioned that living at home was becoming more commonplace among students and younger adults in the U.S., too, given our economic problems.

That was when I learned that the unemployment rate in Spain was about twenty per cent, sometimes higher. "My God," I said, "why aren't people out in the streets protesting?" (Coincidentally, a procession of people protesting about something were marching down the other side of the street as I spoke, carrying banners and shouting slogans presumably aimed at the corruption of the government.) Because, Tom replied, the family still functioned in Spain. If you needed a place to live, a relative would probably take you in, even if you were broke. Some people picked up money off the books working for family members, and if you wanted to look for a job or study in some other part of the country, a relative or family connection could often be found to give you room and board.

In the course of this conversation, I also found out that Spanish primary and secondary schools start classes at 9:00 AM and finish at 5:30 PM. Presumably at least an hour or so is set aside for lunch, but it still seemed like a long day. (On the other hand, the students don't have to get up at ungodly hours to catch school buses, either.) School ends on June 15th and begins again on September 15th.

Eventually we had to leave for dinner (I had followed Rachel's lead and drunk a beverage called Bitter Kas, which tastes like Campari but is non-alcoholic. I wasn't being abstemious, just cautious, knowing that Spanish dinners involve a lot of wine consumption.) Off George and I went with Tom and Rachel in a speeding cab (this driver had to be doing at least eighty miles an hour) to a wonderful restaurant that displayed fresh seafood in its windows and turned out to be a place where they often ate after work; it was basically their neighborhood restaurant, since their apartment was only a few blocks away.

We ate about four different kinds of appetizers, sharing them among ourselves. One was stuffed peppers, and constituted a kind of culinary roulette, since occasionally a pepper was served that would take the roof off your mouth; luckily, I managed to avoid any hot peppers. The main course was shrimp at least three times the size of jumbo shrimp, grilled in a salty but tasty sauce. We had to peel them and eat them by hand, with finger bowls at our sides.

We talked for a long time. One topic that came up was my story featuring the former U.S. Vice President Dan Quayle, "Danny Goes to Mars." (This story of mine had come up before, during my interview for *El País*, when Jacinto Antón had rolled his eyes at the thought of Dan Quayle ever becoming president, and also in discussions with various people after that. Quayle would probably not be reassured to learn that even in Spain, he was widely famed for his vapidity.) I had the feeling that my story was destined to become a cult favorite at the embassy, where the prospect of a Quayle presidency filled people with astonishment that such a possibility even existed. Tom shook his head at the thought of Quayle and his memoir, which had just come out in the U.S. before my departure. "He was just starting his book tour," I told Tom, "when I left." "You should get your publisher to use that to publicize your story!" Tom said. And in fact the Nebula Awards anthology reprinting "Danny Goes to Mars" had come out, coincidentally, at the same time as Quayle's book.

Another subject was writers who refused to bother with promoting their books. Tom mentioned writers who had refused Spanish junkets like mine, who wanted nothing to do with any of the U.S. Information Service programs. Some might simply be terrified of public speaking, but with others it was a matter of principle. "They figure," Tom said, "that the publishers have been screwing them for years, so they'll be damned if they'll lift a finger to help the publisher push their books." I understood, having heard horror stories of a couple of multimillionaire writers who routinely start cursing whenever publishing and editors are mentioned--and those are the *successful* writers.

We found out more about Rachel and Tom. They came from New England, Tom from Worcester, Massachusetts. Before coming to Madrid, they had been stationed at the embassy in Peru and then in Gabon, West Africa. They were in their late thirties and had two children, a daughter who was about four and a son who was fifteen months old, and a woman who had come with them from Peru to look after the kids.

Rachel told me something of her upbringing. She had a way of talking that was like a bird alighting on something, fluttering off, then landing again. She could get into one subject, get distracted by something else, start talking about that, then come back to the earlier subject and pick up where she had left off. She had been educated by nuns in Catholic schools all the way through college. "I was twenty years old," she said, "before I could even talk to a boy without getting nervous!" She had sworn never to put her own daughter through that kind of schooling. I told her that I had gone to a girls' school (granted, a secular girls' school, and not for my whole life, either) and considered it one of the best things that had ever happened to me, that I had my doubts about coeducation. In fact, I said, there were more and more studies indicating that girls thrived intellectually in an all-female environment. Rachel began to reconsider. Her daughter was in a coed pre-school now; was that bad? I assured her that I was no expert on education and as far as I knew, coed primary education was fine; it was when adolescence hit that things got troublesome.

Tom and Rachel would be in Madrid for at least two and a half more years until their next transfer. Where would they go then? They didn't know. "Presumably someplace where Spanish is spoken," I said. "The Foreign Service isn't always that rational," Tom replied. He and Rachel knew French, so Paris would be a good place to be if it came to that. Luckily, since they had put in a certain number of years abroad already, they had a kind of veto power; if somebody wanted to station them in Sarajevo or Mogadishu, they could refuse that assignment. The worst-case scenario, Tom told us, is that they would end up back in Washington, D.C. Why was *that* the worst? I asked. He and Rachel wanted their kids to have good language training, to grow up multilingual, and knew how much harder that would be to do back home. Maybe they also wanted to keep them away from massive doses of American popular culture a little longer, since plenty of our cultural influence had already seeped into Spain as it was.

The subject of bullfighting came up. George mentioned that we had seen bullfights being broadcast on TV. Rachel clearly found the sport reprehensible. That spike stuck into the bull just before he enters the ring is a big, long metal deal guaranteed to cause pain to the animal. "Do you know what the word 'matador' means?" Rachel asked. "Killer!" she went on before George could come out with the answer. No euphemisms there; that's exactly what "matador" means. Thinking of American animal rights groups, I asked Rachel if there were any people in Spain who ever protested against bullfights. "Some people follow the bullfights," she replied, "and other people don't care for them at all and don't go. But nobody protests against them. Even people who don't like them wouldn't dream of trying to prevent them." In all her time in Spain, she had never heard of anyone speaking out against bullfighting, and certainly never of any organized protest.

It was sometime around midnight by the time we left the restaurant. We couldn't stay up too late; I was scheduled to give my talk at the Complutense University of Madrid at 9:30 AM, which qualifies almost as the crack of dawn by Spanish standards. Rachel's parting words were: "I always say, you're only alive once, so you might as well really enjoy yourself!" Even though expressed by an American, it was a very Spanish sentiment. Off Tom and Rachel went in one cab, while George and I headed off in our cab toward the hotel.

I finally managed to sleep, but remember lying for a while in the darkness, before sleep finally came, trying to compose some sort of opening to the extemporaneous speech that Juan Nuñez expected me to give.

WEDNESDAY, MAY 11, 1994

We had already worked out our schedule for the day with Tom the night before. I would give my talk at the University, then come back to the hotel in plenty of time to pack and meet Carlos Aganzo of *YA*, assuming he showed up on time, at one o'clock. After the interview, we would check out of our room, store our bags with the hotel, eat lunch, and then go to the train station by cab to take the 5:00 train to Zaragoza. Tom would be coming up to Zaragoza the next morning, in time to hear my speech there.

We ate an early breakfast and met Tom and Macarena Moreno in the lobby at about 8:45. I had brought along my large folder with all my speeches. "This is my security blanket," I explained to Tom. "I know Professor Nuñez expects me to talk off the top of my head, but I'll feel better if I have *something* in front of me."

The weather didn't look good as we left the hotel, and that was odd for Madrid. The sky had clouded up, the temperature had dropped, and there was a possibility of rain. It practically never rains in Madrid, and at its high altitude, the air is usually dry as a bone, so this weather was definitely uncharacteristic.

The Complutense University of Madrid is part of a university that may be one of the largest in the world (if not the largest); some 500,000 students study there. The university complex is some distance from the center of town, and as we zipped along toward it in our cab, we suddenly came to a wide expanse of grassy and apparently undeveloped land. "This was the front line," Macarena told us, "during the Civil War." This stretch of land was where the Loyalists had made their last stand against Franco in the defense of Madrid. To this day, Macarena went on, people were still discovering caches of weapons buried in the ground—some rifles and ammo had been dug up just the other week.

The building where I was to speak was a structure in a style I've come to think of as "State University of New York Moderne," although the campus itself had a large plaza and grassy spaces between the buildings. Juan Nuñez met us and took us up one flight to the room where I was to speak, then to his office; I could tell that this speech, like the others, was destined to begin about fifteen minutes late. Juan was anxious that I not disappoint his students. They were so looking forward to my talk! Their expectations were so high! If he kept up this line of gab, I thought to myself, I would be in a state of total hysteria when it was time to face my audience.

I was also introduced to Juan's colleague, Professor Isabel Durán, who was to be my other host here. If Dr. Durán ever decides to give up teaching in a university, she could definitely find work as a fashion model; she was drop-dead beautiful, with thick long black hair, lovely brown eyes, a perfect high-cheekboned face, and emaciated figure. I was beginning to think that any American men who despair of finding beautiful women who are also brilliant, articulate, and intellectually stimulating should go to Spain, where they could (judging by the women I had seen so far at universities) meet them in abundance.

Off we went to the big room where I was to speak. Again I was warned that the students might not ask any questions. I parked myself behind the table at the front of the room, spread out my speeches in front of me, and hoped I wouldn't be forced to rely on one of them after all. Juan introduced me, and he had brought a copy of my story from *Asimov y sus amigos* so that he could read a few lines to the audience. He read, then glanced at me. "Perhaps, even in the Spanish, you recognize a few of your lines?" he asked. I shook my head. "I studied French," I admitted, "not Spanish." "You studied the wrong language!" he exclaimed. "I think you're right," I replied. This got everybody laughing, at least, and then I began my speech.

Somehow, I pulled it together. I began with how I had begun to write, moving on to discoveries I had made about the process, what I had learned along the way. Some of the things I had mentioned in my other speeches found their way into this one when they seemed relevant. My security blanket of pages lay in front of me, but I didn't look at them. It was then that I realized that Juan Nuñez had actually done me a favor by facing me with this challenge; I was discovering that I could give a speech without notes.

There were plenty of questions afterward, and later, as we wandered to a lounge area for coffee, Juan told me that I had *not* disappointed his students.

As we sat around with our coffee, Isabel Durán, who was dying to get her hands on a copy of my book (it turned out that one of her specialties was historical fiction), mentioned an upcoming conference on the historical novel that was to be held a couple of weeks later. Pablo had mentioned this conference at some point, but I had forgotten all about it until Isabel brought it up. Apparently professors from all over Spain were going to be there, because there was a big boom in historical fiction in that country. (This was in notable contrast to the U.S., where an editor told me after I got back that there seemed to be no large mass market American audience for historical fiction at that time; all people wanted to read in the U.S. was historical romances.) In the meantime, George and Juan were engrossed in conversation, and ended up really hitting it off. It turned out that Juan was an old leftist who, like a lot of us, was feeling ideologically adrift. He also explained what he had meant by saying that I had studied the wrong language. French was fine if you wanted to read French literature, but with Spanish, you could get around in a lot of different places, including most of Central and South America. And there was a general impression in Spain that Latinos were becoming much more influential in the U.S., and that therefore Spanish was also useful there. (I had to agree with him. If I were going to advise any fellow Americans on what languages to learn nowadays, the three most important seem to be English, Spanish, and Mandarin.)

All too soon, we had to leave, since George and I still had to pack before my interview. Tom made a phone call for a cab, since there was less chance of running into one out there, and then we went outside to meet it on the other side of the plaza. The weather, for the moment at least, had turned sunny.

There were political graffiti all over this campus, just as there had been in Santiago, and one slogan appeared especially popular; it had been spray-painted on the side of the building where I spoke and even on the back of the base of a sculpture of the much-admired founder of the university. George tried to translate it, but one word escaped him. Tom consulted with Macarena, then gave us the translation, which was:

WE ARE EUROPEANS
NOT FASCIST ASSHOLES

* * * *

Tom and Macarena left us at the hotel. We wouldn't see Tom until he arrived in Zaragoza, since he had a lot of work to do at the embassy. So did Macarena, who among her other duties had to tend to the social schedule of the ambassador's wife, a job she found tedious, boring, and also overly complicated. But Macarena would come by to take us to the train station later (I promised, since she was small and slight, that we would carry our own bags), and Tom assured us that Professor Francisco Collado, who was to meet us in Zaragoza, was extremely reliable. "I'll fax him this afternoon," Tom said, "just to double-check," and then it dawned on him that Professor Collado had no idea of what we looked like.

"That's okay," I said. "Just tell him to look for a woman with big wild hair and a man with a carved wooden cane and a Panama hat." Tom burst out laughing at that, and replied: "There won't be anybody else on the train fitting that description!"

We went back to our room, and I was just finishing my packing when the phone rang; George answered it. Carlos Aganzo had arrived, fifteen minutes early this time. Down George and I went to meet him, since my interpreter Blanca Novo wasn't due there until one.

Carlos Aganzo turned out to be a tall and sturdily built young bruiser with a black beard and enough knowledge of English to utter heartfelt apologies for the screwup of the day before. He was so sorry! He hoped I didn't think badly of him! How relieved he was that I would still consent to an interview! His photographer was with him—he gestured at a man carrying photographic equipment—so perhaps we could take photos while waiting for my interpreter.

We went out to the patio adjoining the sitting area, since the sun had come out, which made it the perfect spot for picture-taking. Our timing was perfect; just as the photographer was finishing up, the sky started clouding up once more. I went back upstairs to phone Blanca at the embassy, to make sure that she was on her way, and also to throw my last unpacked toilet articles into my suitcase. In the meantime, George practiced his Spanish with Carlos Aganzo, and found out from the journalist that he had learned his limited English by watching American movies.

By the time I got back to the lobby, Blanca had arrived, so we retreated to the patio while George left to finish his packing. The man from *Ya* asked questions about my Genghis Khan book, about science fiction, and about a host of other subjects I'd talked about before, so I was able to give him good answers, and Blanca turned out to be an excellent interpreter. Mr. Aganzo was especially interested in my opinion of the growing cultural influence of Hispanic-Americans in the U.S. (My opinion was that it was the diversity of our culture, and the effect that different ethnic groups have upon it, that keeps it vital.) He was also fascinated by the notion that there were places one could now visit in the U.S. where you didn't have to know English and could get by with Spanish, although he seemed to believe that there were many more such places than there actually are. (About five days after I got back home, Tom Leary faxed me a copy of the printed *Ya* interview.)

After exchanging pleasantries with Blanca and Mr. Aganzo, I went back upstairs, and then George and I went through the business of checking out, storing luggage, and eating lunch, about which there is little to say except that we had excellent service and the food (soup, a Spanish variation on a salad Niçoise, hard rolls, and wine) was delicious.

* * * *

We got to the train station with Macarena at about four; our train was to leave at five. The train station looked a bit run-down, and Macarena warned us to be careful of thieves and not to wander away from our luggage. But in fact this terminal seemed relatively safe, with ordinary citizens sitting around in the waiting area. "Madrid-Zaragoza-Pam" read the listing for our train; it was because the last stop was Pamplona, not because I was taking it. Macarena stayed with us until the platform number for our train was posted, then left to go back to work.

I knew only a little about Spanish trains. The government run-train system, RENFE, was supposed to be pretty bad, definitely below the standards of the rest of Europe. I had heard stories that the trains weren't any too comfortable, either, although the TALGO high-speed trains were nicer. We weren't going to be on a TALGO for this leg of the trip, just one of the older choo-choos, but Zaragoza was only three hours away by train, and we had wanted to see more of the countryside.

We got down to our platform on an escalator and, after consulting the seat numbers on our tickets, found the proper car. At this point, we discovered that the simplest way to get our luggage aboard was to throw it through the door and then climb in after it. We entered a car which, to my untutored eye, looked like a perfectly respectable train; in fact, it looked considerably nicer than the Amtrak job George and I had taken to Florida from New York some years earlier. The seats were about the same size as those on Greyhound buses, so we were a bit cramped, but the car was air-conditioned and the ride relatively smooth. I'm also pretty sure that we were the only Americans, and possibly the only foreigners, on it.

Off the train went, chugging toward Madrid's outskirts. We passed high-rise apartment buildings near the edge of the city, and then had our first real glimpse of Spanish poverty. We had seen a few poor people in Barcelona going through garbage cans and dumpsters in the side streets, and some of the street people along La Rambla looked frayed around the edges, but here, outside the city, was where much of the poverty was. Americans tended to move out, leaving rotting urban centers behind, while Spaniards tended to crowd into a city's center. Outside Madrid we saw wretched-looking trailer parks, shacks, and hovels that looked as though they might cave in at any moment. There was, not surprisingly, a lot of graffiti on various walls and surfaces.

As the train moved north, the land got progressively more arid. Madrid and the plateau on which it is located are dry, but there were trees and greenery, farms and orchards there, even if some of the hillsides had wide red gashes and other signs of erosion. The farther north we went, the more barren and dramatic the landscape became. About one and half hours out of Madrid, we were crossing wide expanses of dry land and desert, with rocky cliffs and mesas jutting up from the ground, that looked exactly like the American West. Monument Valley! I thought. The clear bright blue sky was almost painful to look at, and the desolation had the kind of familiar stark beauty I had seen in countless Westerns. There was one difference, though.

On top of several of these gray stone precipices were castles and fortresses surrounded by high thick walls.

Spain, as we were discovering, is a country of varied geography, almost as varied as that of the U.S., even if the country isn't as big.

We were moving through Aragon, the province in which Zaragoza is located. We were going through what was, for most tourists anyway, relatively unknown territory; even *Fodor's Spain* had little to say about Aragon, and nothing at all about Zaragoza. We weren't exactly going to have much time to explore it, either, since we had to take a train to Barcelona the next day at around two in the afternoon.

The train reached Zaragoza's station on time, at about 8:15 PM. We had stashed our bags in a luggage compartment at one end of our car; since we were schlepping more luggage than the other passengers, we waited before grabbing our own stuff. The simplest way—indeed, the only way—to get off the train in the three minutes we had before it took off for Pamplona, given the narrow step down and the distance we had to jump to the platform, was to hurl our bags out forcefully and then leap after them, which we did.

We were the last ones off the train. The other passengers were moving toward the escalators and exits. Some fifty feet from us stood the lone figure of a casually but nattily dressed man carrying a large shopping bag. My guess was that this was Professor Collado.

He walked toward us, and was clearly relieved to find out that we were the people he was supposed to meet. "I thought you might have missed the train," he said. Francisco Collado, who was about my height, had short black hair, designer glasses, a fine-featured pale scholarly-looking face, and a manner of speaking that made him sound like Peter Sellers in the role of Inspector Clouseau. I was soon to discover that he was both a card and extremely fluent in English, so fluent that he picked up on everything, including slang and idiomatic expressions, which were delicacies he savored. Never once did I have to explain what I meant. It also wasn't long before we were calling him by his nickname, Paco, despite his full formal name and title of Dr. Francisco Collado Rodríguez.

We took a cab into Zaragoza, which Paco said had a population of about 700,000 people. Despite its size and its history, it still seemed a bit off the beaten track, except that just about everybody, it seemed, had come through Zaragoza over the centuries. It was over two thousand years old, starting out as a Roman city. Since then, it had been conquered at various times by Franks (under Charlemagne), Arabs (who ruled in Zaragoza for a couple of hundred years), and assorted Spanish and French armies, and a lot of this was evident in its architecture. There were Roman ruins, medieval walls, and edifices that had once been parts of mosques. This was El Cid territory, even if he did eventually end up on the coast in Valencia, and in fact the epic motion picture *El Cid*, starring Charlton Heston and Sophia Loren, had been filmed south of Zaragoza and in some of the areas we had seen from our train.

There were also, of course, plenty of modern structures, and lots of traffic in Zaragoza. The main thoroughfares were wide, but the side streets were the familiar narrow European city alleyways, which didn't prevent cars and taxis from barreling through them. Our hotel was a four-star place called the Hotel Goya, located along a narrow street off one of the main plazas and traffic circles. Even though the hotel had been named for the great artist, the sitting room off the lobby had only a faded reproduction of "The Clothed Maja." ("If they were going to put that one up," George commented, "they should have put up the nude, too.") In spite of its four stars, we were to find that the Hotel Goya was a lot like an American motel; it was the least atmospheric of our Spanish hostelries.

Paco checked us in, then presented me with the shopping bag, which turned out to contain a gift-wrapped present and a colorful folder full of maps and guides to the city. He was very sorry I couldn't stay longer in Zaragoza. It seemed to be his fate, he went

---

ABOUT ZARAGOZA

Zaragoza was a Roman colony founded in the time of Augustus and sited along the Ebro River. From 714 until 1118, it was ruled by the Moors, then conquered by a Christian army after that. It was, during medieval times, a cultural center with a rich intellectual life, a city where Muslims, Christians, and Jews lived peacefully together. That period of tolerance was to end in Spain when Christian armies had reconquered all of the country, and when the Jews were expelled in 1492.

on, to have the few American visitors who passed this way stay only briefly in his little part of the world. He was so courtly about all of this that I was soon making solemn pledges that I would come back there on a return visit.

George and I went upstairs to unpack. Paco was to meet us in the lobby at around nine-thirty and take us to dinner. Our room was perfectly comfortable, and had all the requisite facilities (except air-conditioning, which we didn't really need), but it was dark and almost creepy; you could imagine Goya having a nightmare in this place and then doing one of his "black paintings." George ascertained that CNN International News wasn't among the TV channels here, and then I unwrapped my present, which turned out to be a beautiful book of photographs showing different parts of Zaragoza. I was touched!

We went downstairs, found Paco in the lobby, where I thanked him for his gifts and again swore mighty oaths that I would return to Zaragoza, and we were soon outside walking down a side street in the cool but dry air of the evening. Some interesting Roman ruins weren't far away, so Paco was going to pick a restaurant near them. What kind of food were we looking for? Anything that's local, I told him, food that's characteristic of the region.

Paco knew just the place. It turned out to be down a wide, darkened street where not many people seemed to be out walking. "About a year ago," Paco murmured in his Inspector Clouseau voice, "it wouldn't have been safe to come here at night. All the gangs used to hang out around here, the drug dealers, and there was a lot of violence, people getting beaten up and shot." I looked around nervously. "What happened?" I asked. "The police came in," he answered, "made a sweep, confiscated the weapons, arrested everybody, and told the people they couldn't hold to get out of town. Maybe they all went back to Barcelona!" Since this effort at urban renewal, new businesses had come into the area, which was beginning to prosper.

The restaurant was on the second floor of a building housing a hotel, and I went into raptures when we entered the dining room. The walls were covered with painted tiles, there was a fireplace (without a fire, since the weather was mild), the tables were covered with fine linen tablecloths, the chairs were sturdy high-backed ones with arms; El Cid wouldn't have minded chowing down there. The only drawback to the place was that the chef (judging by the muted sounds of the music emanating from the kitchen) was a Led Zeppelin fan, which meant listening to "Stairway to Heaven" and other Led Zeppelin classics more times than I care to remember. As for what sort of food is characteristic of the region, it's meat on the table in Aragon; the specialties are lamb and beef--marinated, grilled, and in large portions. Among our appetizers, which we shared, were tuna and shrimp dishes and more stuffed peppers with which one had to play culinary roulette.

Paco was extremely apologetic about the Spanish trains. They were terrible, he told us, and he had feared that we might be very uncomfortable. I told him we'd had a great time on the choo-choo, that we had wanted to see more of the country, and that anyway we were used to American trains. "American trains!" he said with a shudder, and went on to speak of his first trip on the Long Island Rail Road, which he had made less than a year before on a visit to New York, a city that he loves. He had been going out of the city to see a friend on Long Island, and the train trip, as he put it, was like traveling on a roller coaster; it was the worst train he had ever been on in his life.

Here's something to consider: Amtrak (I found this out from Tom Leary later) was then thinking of buying a few of Spain's TALGO trains for a pilot project, while Spain is already working to upgrade its whole system to high-speed trains. We were at least a decade behind them, maybe more, and Spain allegedly had the worst trains in Europe. George and I, on our junket to Zaragoza, had been traveling on the Spanish equivalent of a Greyhound bus, since trains were basically the way the less well-off traveled in Spain. In other words, the U.S. at that point probably had some of the worst trains in the world. As for plane travel within the country, Paco told me that Iberia and Aviaco had retired their propeller jobs, ones like the plane that had flown us out of Binghamton (and like the planes then used by lots of commuter airlines over here), years ago, and used only jet aircraft now. All of which leads me to think that there are some benefits to having government-subsidized train and plane travel. We'll never have it, of course, because we put so much of our money into highways.

We talked a lot. Paco, it turned out, had been delighted to snag me for an appearance in front of his students, and said that his colleague, Dr. Susana Onega, was sure to show up. "She was a feminist here twenty years ago, before anyone else was," he exclaimed admiringly. He insisted that he didn't know all that much about American science fiction, then went on to demonstrate with some of the authors he cited that he actually had some grasp of the field. When Paco found out I had been to Santiago, but had missed meeting Professor Constante Gonzalez, he expressed regret. "He's so funny," Paco said. "He's got a great sense of humor. I can't talk to him without laughing." Paco, it turned out, had done his military service near Santiago, and it didn't sound as though it was one of his favorite places in the world, but he had nothing but praise for Dr. Gonzalez.

The subject of politics came up. "Americans think," Paco said, "that if they find someone virtuous, and put him in office, that he will reform and change the system, that it's only a matter of finding the right person. We call it the American dream, because it is only a dream." I told him that things might be changing. After President Richard Nixon cashed in his chips that spring, I pointed out, there were several stories about the reaction of U.S. teenagers and young people to the media's coverage of his life and death, and the vast majority of the young people interviewed were completely cynical. Their attitude was that all politicians were corrupt, on the take, and interested only in perpetuating their own power, so why had everyone gotten so upset with Nixon? He was no worse than all the others, in their mind. Paco smiled, as if thinking: Americans are finally learning what the world's like. At the same time, he was very surprised that President Clinton and other political leaders had actually made a kind of state event out of Nixon's funeral. That, he asserted, would never have happened in Spain. The man had left office in disgrace, and it didn't seem fitting to have other leaders, especially Clinton, who had protested Nixon's policies in his youth, turn out to honor him at his funeral.

Americans did have their own traditions of political cynicism, I pointed out; I had grown up in Albany, New York, after all. Paco's ears pricked up. William Kennedy had passed through Zaragoza the previous autumn, and had entertained Paco with all kinds of Albany lore, but I was able (thanks to my father, who told me the story) to tell a tale Paco hadn't yet heard. It was the story of Dan O'Connell, the powerful boss of Albany's Democratic machine for decades, and the Citizens Party, which I'll summarize. A group of people wanting reform had founded the Citizens Party (this was in the early 1960s), and were soon running candidates in local elections. One of their candidates even became Mayor of Cohoes. The Democratic Party faithful around Dan O'Connell urged him to put a stop to this, something that was well within his power, since several of the Citizens Party members were Democrats, but old Dan was too sly for that. He let the Citizens Party continue, more and more Democrats hoping for reform went public in backing the new party, and within a few years the Citizens Party had completely collapsed and Dan O'Connell knew who his enemies were, since they had been suckered into going out in the open with their support of the Citizens Party. It was exactly the same tactic Mao Tse-tung had used in his One Hundred Flowers campaign in China during the 1950s. Paco liked that story.

Paco had been in the U.S. on various occasions, and one aspect of American life he found especially dismal was that everything shut down so early. He spoke of a time he had traveled to Oxford, Mississippi, reaching the town at about nine at night on a bus. "Everything was closed," he said. "I was ready to have dinner and go out for the night, and everything was closed! It happens all over your country. There's no place to go after nine-thirty or ten. It's very depressing." Given that staying out all night is a traditional Spanish thing, his reaction wasn't surprising.

All of us talked about publishing, literature, and various other subjects until past midnight, and the streets seemed pretty empty by the time we got outside. About the only other people we saw just outside the restaurant were a bunch of teenaged soccer players and their coach, probably on their way home after a game. This was when I began to get the feeling that Zaragoza, despite its history, its 700,000 people, and a multitude of bars, cafes, and discos that stayed open until five in the morning, was something of a cow town, which seemed to be the way Paco regarded the place, too.

I was supposed to speak at the university at 11:00 AM, but Paco was going to come by and pick us up at around nine-thirty, since he was going to meet Tom at the train station and it would be easier for us all to head out to the university after George and I were checked out and our luggage stored. Fine with me! By that point, I'd had enough wine to sleep soundly when we got back to the hotel.

THURSDAY, MAY 12, 1994

I dragged myself out of bed early, knowing I would have to make myself presentable, get some coffee and breakfast into me, and pack my stuff before Paco and Tom arrived. George decided that an extra forty minutes or so of sleep were more important to him than breakfast, so I went to the downstairs dining room alone. The buffet offered rolls, croissants, fruit, meats and cheeses (I snagged the last piece of Jabon ham), and scrambled eggs. The only other people eating at that hour were a couple of middle-aged Spanish men and a table full of British men in business suits. A grim-faced young waitress with the demeanor of a prison guard brought me my coffee, and getting a second cup from her required waving my arms around and using my Spanish phrase book; I had grown too accustomed to classy, silent, automatic service. From the kitchen, I could hear the sounds of Metallica and Judas Priest ("You got another thing coming!"). There seemed to be a lot of heavy metal fans in Zaragoza.

I had time after breakfast to take a walk and look at some of the nearby sights. The sky was blue and cloudless, as usual. I kept stopping at newsstands, since the Hotel Goya only had copies of the Spanish papers, but couldn't find an *International Herald Tribune* anywhere, or any other English-language paper. There were places around the traffic circle where, if there was a break in the traffic and some ensuing silence, I could almost feel that I was in an ancient city, since much of the new has been built around the old remnants of mosques, synagogues, and Roman ruins.

I finally headed back to the hotel, George and I called a porter to take our bags downstairs, and by then Paco and Tom had shown up. We piled into a cab and headed toward the university, a seat of learning that's been around since medieval times. A lot of construction was going on there, and the building housing Paco's office and the room where I was to speak was a big new glassy structure. Paco pointed out all the posters heralding my appearance; he had had them made up in different sizes and colors and plastered them just about everywhere, on bulletin boards, walls, stairwells, and near other posters advertising a lecture about Charles Bukowski. (Before I left, he gave me a few of my posters as souvenirs.)

George was still without breakfast and needed a caffeine infusion. Paco said we could go either to the faculty cafeteria, which he considered quite gloomy and depressing, or a student cafeteria in a building across the way that was more disorderly but less gloomy. So off we went to the student place, where we all had coffee but couldn't find a place to sit, since students had taken all of the tables. We stood near the bar (there was a bar there, with beer, wine, and hard liquor, and a few people were drinking at that hour) and talked. Paco was telling Tom what he had told me before—namely, that he was extremely angry with a few of his colleagues, who had suddenly scheduled their final exams for this week. There was absolutely no reason to schedule them that early, and he hinted that these fellow professors were thinking only of their own convenience, since they could end their classes sooner that way. What worried him was that people who might otherwise have come to my speech would be studying for exams, and that I wouldn't have much of an audience. I tried to reassure Paco, as I had before, that I wouldn't be insulted if the audience was small; I had given a reading years before where only two people had shown up. But Paco, in his restrained way, was furious; that much I could tell.

We went back to Paco's office and met his colleague Susana Onega, who was delighted to hear that I had finished editing two new *Women of Wonder* anthologies (she had seen *Mujeres y maravillas*, a Spanish edition of the first *WoW* that had been published ages ago there). With her was a British feminist colleague, whose name completely escaped me, maybe because by then Paco was urging us all in the direction of the room where I was to speak. He would introduce me and, as he told me, be my "inquisitor" afterward. This wasn't the best choice of words, but Paco had a well-developed sense of irony.

Exams or not, the room filled up, and once again, people asked questions after the speech was over. I was speaking on "Women and Science Fiction" again, since Paco and Susana Onega had specifically requested a lecture on that topic, but this time I adlibbed more. (I guess that worked; Tom, who had heard much the same speech at the Casa de America, said that he got even more out of it this time.)

Paco asked me one question in particular that struck me. "I know that now there are some divisions among women writers in your country," he said, "that some are more interested in drawing on their African-American experience, Native American past, lesbianism, or whatever, and aren't as concerned with women and feminism in general. Is this true in science fiction? Do you have similar divisions and disputes among yourselves?" (This tendency, which was becoming increasingly common among writers of all sorts, has sometimes been referred to as "the Balkanization of literature.") I admitted that we didn't in science fiction, at least not yet, because a lot of the writers are happy to be writing in a form that doesn't limit them to being only a certain kind of writer. "Octavia Butler," I told him, "doesn't have to write only about the kinds of things a Black writer would be expected to write about. Samuel R. Delany doesn't just have to be a gay writer. They can make use of who and what they are in their work without being limited only to that." Unfortunately, I went on, another sadder reason we didn't have so many divisions is that there weren't that many writers of diverse backgrounds in science fiction yet; it was still largely a white (and male) field.

One thing had become clear to me during this trip. Whatever our own more complicated feelings about the women's movement were (and I admitted that there had been a backlash and more ambivalent feelings about the women's movement in the U.S.), there were women in Spain who still looked to feminism for inspiration. Maybe that's not surprising. "Macho" and "machismo" are, after all, Spanish words.

I stood around talking to people for a while, and then Paco led us back to his office. My train for Barcelona left at 2:08 PM, according to the schedule, which meant too little time to hang around and schmooze. Paco was pleased enough with my speech to ask for permission to publish it in English in an academic journal his department was doing, and Tom said that the Casa de America people wanted to do it in Spanish. No problem! Paco went off to make a quick photocopy, then returned to explain to George how he had come by the nickname of Paco. It seems a famous Spanish poet whose first name was Francisco had signed his poems with a pseudonym that, over the centuries, had been shortened to "Paco." So now, as Paco put it, all Franciscos are Pacos. Politics came up, as it had a habit of doing. Tom had seen a debate in the Spanish parliament on TV the night before, and had been amazed at how savagely and angrily some members had questioned the prime minister. Paco murmured that the Spanish parliament seemed to be taking more and more lessons in deportment from the British parliament—and anyone who has seen "Question Time" on C-Span knows that the British House of Commons members are masters of sarcasm and dissing of prime ministers.

Tom called the embassy to tell somebody to make sure that Le Meridien in Barcelona wasn't going to leave us stranded without a room somewhere, and then off we went to look for a cab. There didn't seem to be any near the university, so Paco and I were soon scouting ahead while George and Tom dropped behind.

Paco was sorry I was leaving so soon. So was I, and swore another blood oath that I would return. By coming at this time of the year, he said, I had also deprived myself of one typical Spanish experience—lying around on the beach all day in the summertime. (Apparently nobody worries much about ultraviolet rays.) We passed a newsstand, where various skin rags were on sale among the newspapers. "After Franco died," Paco said, "everybody went sex mad." "In other words," I said, "the lid was off." "Exactly!" he murmured. Paco went on to make an admission. "I hate cars," he told me. "I will have nothing to do with them." I informed him that I hated them myself and did not drive, in spite of being an American. "It's crazy," he said. "I don't understand how Americans can spend twenty minutes driving to work. It's such a waste of time! They could be spending it reading, with their friends, enjoying themselves, and they're stuck driving the car." I told him that a lot of people in my country would be happy if it took them only twenty minutes to get to work, that there were people who commuted forty minutes to an hour one way or even more. He shook his head at such irrationality and insanity. Then I learned that Paco had a dream—a very American dream, as it happened. He hated cars, but he also hated noise. One thing he hated about living in the middle of Zaragoza was that there was never any peace and quiet. His dream was to get an apartment, maybe even a house, on the outskirts of town or in the countryside. There didn't seem much chance of that happening, though, because his wife loved living in the center of town and didn't want to move. "But wouldn't you have to get a car if you moved?" I asked. Apparently not; he would still be on a bus route, with a bus coming along every ten minutes.

We eventually came to a cab stand, and were soon heading back to the hotel. There was time enough for George to get a sandwich (since he still hadn't had anything to eat) at a nearby cafe. Tom and Paco got beers, and I settled for bottled water and a couple of tapas, one with tuna and one with shrimp. Paco disapproved of the fact that this place charged people for the little appetizers instead of serving them free with drinks, but lots of places were beginning to charge separately for tapas now. Another deplorable new development in Spanish life, according to Paco.

Tom was in Zaragoza not just on my account, but because he had business of some sort to discuss with Paco—he was also there, I suspect, because they were good friends and this was a good excuse to get together. They were going to have lunch together as soon as George and I were aboard our train. I was feeling slightly melancholy. There weren't any more speeches to give, so that pressure was off; the problem was that I would have to go home soon and deal with all my professional and financial problems.

We went back to the Hotel Goya, collected our luggage, and went off to the train station. We were going to be on a TALGO this time, one of the high-speed trains. When we got to our platform, Tom warned us that we would have only four minutes to get aboard. Spanish trains were very much on time, especially the high-speed ones, and wouldn't wait even a few seconds for passengers who were too slow.

We said our farewells. "You will not have to worry about the security guards at the airport," Paco said. "They will be too busy looking for their boss," namely the National Guard head who had absconded with millions from the treasury. The train pulled in, we hurled our bags aboard with all our might, and clambered aboard with about a minute to spare.

(A few days after returning home, I got a letter from Paco. He was getting ready to publish my speech, told me I must stay longer in Zaragoza next time, said he enjoyed his conversations with George and me about "this crazy world" and added mysteriously that when I returned, "La Posada de las Animas will be waiting for you...'spirits' are still okay in this country...")

****

The train was taking us east through flat, dry, Arizona-type land, but to the north, we could see the Pyrenees in the distance. They made me think of huge giant pointed grayish-blue teeth jutting toward the sky. They had to be a good fifty miles or so away, but the land was so flat that we could see them easily.

The TALGO train had bigger windows, larger seats, and more leg room than our earlier train. We also had a much smoother ride; no bumps and no swaying. A couple of hours into the trip, two porters came down the aisle with sandwiches, beer, wine, soda, and snacks, so it wasn't necessary to head for the club car. Just as well, since the club car, as we had found out on the other train, was usually packed.

This route would take us south, then up along the coast to Barcelona. The train would be barreling along soundlessly (TALGO trains are quiet, too), and then slow as it came toward a scheduled stop, where it usually remained for no more than four minutes before humming and taking off once more. On the walls and sides of buildings next to the tracks, plenty of graffiti artists had been at work; there were slogans all over the place, spray-painted in bright colors. Why paint them here? I wondered. Maybe just because, as George speculated, it would be easy for people on trains to read them.

The last part of the trip was memorable, and of particular interest to George, because he had always wanted to write a novel about the Carthaginian general Hannibal. He had discussed this ambition with Pablo Somarriba earlier, and Pablo had given him a copy of a historical novel about Hannibal that Edhasa had published. (The novel's in Spanish, and since it doesn't look as though it'll be out in English any time soon, George has an excuse to work on his Spanish some more.) The Carthaginians had been in Spain even before the Romans, and now we were traveling up the Mediterranean coast toward Tarragona, the same route Hannibal had once taken. Suddenly, on our right, there were beaches covered with pale sand, palm trees, and then the Mediterranean stretching to the horizon. We saw the occasional trailer park, and some broken-down old shacks, but also pale high-rise buildings that resembled the condominiums in Miami Beach. The closer we came to Barcelona, the more the condo complexes seemed to predominate; there was a lot of money in those buildings. We didn't see many people, but it wasn't yet the season for vacations and beaches. People would be swarming there from all over Europe that summer.

We got to the Barcelona station that was our stop at about six-thirty, and were able to drop our bags on the platform instead of hurling them through the door; our car's steps were closer to the platform, making it a lot easier to get off the train. With no trouble at all, we found a cart for our luggage, followed the signs to an exit, and located a line of taxis.

We didn't have far to go to Le Meridien. Along the way, an impetuous motorcyclist darted in front of our cab, nearly got hit by our driver, then took up a position alongside the cab when the driver began to curse at him loudly. "What's he saying?" I asked George. "That the other guy is no more than a turd on the road," George replied. "You know, stuff like that." We went on like that for about five long blocks, with the cabdriver and the motorcyclist barreling along side by side while shouting curses at each other. We came to the familiar streets around the Plaça Catalunya. I had seen this city for the first time only the week before, but this was almost like coming home.

We got out at Le Meridien, the doorman and a porter carried our bags inside, and then the concierge on duty came to the desk to tell us that they were still booked solid with no cancellations and had not been able to find us a room. We were, however, not to worry. She was on the phone right now with other hotels, and would have something for us in only a few minutes.

The concierge was as good as her word. She, George and I, and two bellhops carrying our bags and all the stuff we had left at Le Meridien the week before, were soon setting off in a procession down the narrow side street to the Hotel Ambassador, which was only a block away. The concierge hung around long enough to apologize again for any inconvenience before she left. To my mind, it was an awfully minor inconvenience.

The Hotel Ambassador turned out to be a four-star job with most of the comforts anyone would demand. Our room was considerably smaller than the one at Le Meridien, and the beds were two slightly oversized twin beds pushed together rather than one that was king-sized. But we had a small sitting area and a little outside balcony where we could sit and relax. The bathroom yielded yet another treasure, a huge sunken bathtub with a Jacuzzi. We would be able to administer some therapy to our aching bones before enduring the long trans-Atlantic flight.

We had promised to call Pablo when we got in, so we did, trying first his office and then his home. The babysitter answered his home phone, and since she couldn't speak any English, and George wasn't quite sure what to tell her, he left his name, hoping that might be enough. Around 8:30, we tried again. By this time, George had prepared a simple statement in Spanish saying that we were at the Hotel Ambassador and would be there until it was time to go to dinner. We went outside to enjoy the balcony, then realized we would have to rustle up some supper soon; Pablo, for all we knew, might not get home until midnight. So George left another message at Pablo's home saying we had gone out but would be back later, and I left a written one at the desk with the concierge to read to Pablo if he called.

We set off toward La Rambla. The birdsellers were out, the newsstands still open, and the mimes were going about their business. I loved this city. Madrid had won my respect, but Barcelona had my heart.

We headed up toward the Cafe Zurich and then down the street that led to the university. A big bookstore, oddly named Happy Books (it was apparently one of a chain of bookstores in Barcelona) was still open, so we went in to scope the place out--and there, near the front of the store, among the novels, I saw my book, *Gengis Kan: El soberano del cielo*, for sale. Whoa, I thought, and hung around staring at it for a while. They had put my novel in a good spot, right where it would be hard to miss seeing it. A woman came by, and didn't buy it, but stood there staring at it for a few minutes.

We wandered back to La Rambla, along a part of the street we hadn't explored before, then headed up toward Egipte. Somehow, that seemed the right place to go for our last dinner here. The upstairs area filled up not long after we got there, as it had the last time. I ordered what turned out to be an avocado and crabmeat appetizer and something with *gambas* in it that turned out to be a tasty beef relleno rolled around some shrimp. We got a bottle of Cava with the meal, which the waiter parked in an ice bucket, and soon the people at the surrounding tables, including two Scandinavian-looking lesbians, were beaming and smiling sentimentally at us. Maybe they thought we were celebrating our anniversary.

We dawdled outside for as long as we could, breathing in some of our last Barcelona night air, then returned to the Hotel Ambassador to find a message from Pablo. He was glad the trip had gone so well and asked us to call him as soon as we got in. It was at least 11:30 by then, but we knew he would still be up.

He was, sounding as alert as ever. I gave him a brief rundown on how well the trip had gone, and told him I'd seen my book on sale. George got on the phone to exchange a few words. We promised to keep in touch, and to send Pablo some of our other books. Pablo assured me that he would like to see any of my future historical novels, especially one about Russia that I had briefly mentioned to him as a possibility. I'm sure he would have come by to take us to the airport next morning, except that our flight departure time was 11:00 AM, which meant Pablo would have to get up at an ungodly hour to meet us at the hotel. Knowing this, I assured him that we would have no problem getting to the airport by ourselves.

"I've been swearing I'll come back," I told Pablo toward the end of the conversation. "I absolutely have to, as soon as possible." "Come back in two or three weeks!" was his answer. Would that had been possible!

MAY 13, 1994

Somehow we managed to fit all our stuff, including the presents from Pablo, Paco, and the Institute, into our bags. We probably could have found a cab just by going out and heading toward La Rambla to hail one, but it was easier to have the concierge arrange for one over the phone. According to *Fodor's Spain*, a ride to the airport from where we were could take forty minutes, but our cabdriver speeded along and made it in twenty. We were inside the airport terminal by around 9:20. The weather was cloudy and rainy, which made it a little easier to be leaving.

We lined up at the TWA desk to check in. The line was already long, and a security guard, a pretty young woman with long curly black hair, was already questioning passengers. Eventually she came to us. We had to show her our passports and answer a lot of questions. How long were you in the country? What was your address while here? Is all this luggage yours? Did you receive any gifts while in Spain? What were they? Did any strangers try to give you anything to take aboard the plane? What was the purpose of your visit? I had to admit that it was for business purposes, and when she asked what kind of business, George told her. A book tour! This thrilled the security guard. What was my book called, what was it about? I described it briefly, and she made me write down my name and the title so that she could buy a copy. So maybe I sold one copy of *Gengis Kan: El soberano del cielo* on my way out of the country.

What with checking in, and being questioned, we made it to our gate only about fifteen minutes before our flight started boarding. On the way, I hastily unloaded some pesetas at a duty-free shop and bought a lovely handmade fan for what was probably too much money. Still, I got use out of it and dubbed it my menopausal Spanish fan, since it came in handy during hot flashes and was a lot more attractive than waving a magazine or piece of cardboard at my face.

* * * *

There isn't much to say about the flight home. We were on another TWA Lockheed 1101 that had seen better days, and the flight attendants ran out of newspapers before we saw any in our section; the first class and business class passengers snagged them all. The food once again was toy food, but I drank a lot of free wine. We struck up a congenial conversation with the couple behind us, a tall friendly white guy with curly brown hair and a pretty Asian-American woman who seemed madly infatuated with him, and found out they were from Philadelphia. I read about half of William Gibson's cyberpunk classic *Neuromancer*, which I'd brought with me, and discovered that it was the perfect book to read on a plane. Every time I passed through the smoking section in the back on my way to the can, I couldn't help noticing how much livelier it was than non-smoking. People were standing around in the aisles drinking wine, talking over the backs of chairs, and generally acting as though the flight was a social occasion—but then almost all the people in the smoking section were Spanish.

Getting our bags at the carousel in JFK took forty minutes; I was beginning to think TWA had lost them when they finally came zipping down the chute. By the time we were going through customs, I was feeling as though we had returned to the Third World, which is about how JFK seemed after Barcelona. We killed some time in a bar, headed back to the TWA terminal, and sat in a waiting area with all the ambiance of a bus terminal. We finally boarded a commuter plane even tinier than the one we had taken at the beginning of our journey; this plane had only twenty seats. I was dreading this flight, but luckily it was smooth. We landed at the Binghamton airport at about 8:30 in the evening.

The airport was almost empty. We had the airport shuttle van entirely to ourselves. The driver said that the weather had been cloudy and cold, but "it's getting a lot better now. You came back on the best day we've had in a while."

ABOUT PAMELA SARGENT

Pamela Sargent has won the Nebula and Locus Awards, been a finalist for the Hugo Award, Theodore Sturgeon Award, and Sidewise Award, and was honored in 2012 with the SFRA Award for Lifetime Contributions to Science Fiction and Fantasy Scholarship (previously the Pilgrim Award) by the Science Fiction Research Association.

She is the author of the science fiction novels *Cloned Lives*, *The Sudden Star*, *Watchstar*, *The Golden Space*, *The Alien Upstairs*, *Eye of the Comet*, *Homesmind*, *Alien Child*, *The Shore of Women*, *Venus of Dreams*, *Venus of Shadows*, and *Child of Venus*, as well as the alternative history *Climb the Wind*. *Ruler of the Sky*, her 1993 historical novel about Genghis Khan, was a bestseller in Germany and Spain. She also edited the *Women of Wonder* anthologies, the first collections of science fiction by women, published in the 1970s by Vintage/Random House and in updated editions during the 1990s by Harcourt Brace; her other anthologies are *Afterlives*, edited with Ian Watson, *Bio-Futures*, and *Conqueror Fantastic*.

Tor Books reissued her 1983 young adult novel *Earthseed*, selected as a Best Book for Young Adults by the American Library Association, and a sequel, *Farseed*, in early 2007. *Farseed* was chosen by the New York Public Library for their 2008 Books for the Teen Age list of best books for young adults. A third novel, *Seed Seeker*, was published in 2010. *Earthseed* is in development by Paramount Pictures, and her most recent novel is *Season of the Cats*, published in 2015 by Wildside Press.

Sargent sold her first published story as a senior in college at the State University of New York/Binghamton University, where she earned a B.A. and M.A. in philosophy and also studied ancient history and Greek. Her short fiction has appeared in magazines and anthologies including *The Magazine of Fantasy & Science Fiction*, *Asimov's SF Magazine*, *New Worlds*, *World Literature Today*, *Amazing Stories*, *Rod Serling's Twilight Zone Magazine*, *Universe*, *Nature*, and *Polyphony*, and in her collections *Starshadows*, *The Best of*

Pamela Sargent, The Mountain Cage and Other Stories, Behind the Eyes of Dreamers and Other Short Novels, Eye of Flame, Thumbprints, Dream of Venus and Other Science Fiction Stories, and most recently in *Puss in D.C. and Other Stories*, published by Wildside Press in 2015. Her short story "The Shrine" was produced for the syndicated TV anthology series *Tales from the Darkside*, recently re-released on DVD.

Michael Moorcock has said about her writing: "If you have not read Pamela Sargent, then you should make it your business to do so at once. She is in many ways a pioneer, both as a novelist and as a short story writer... She is one of the best."

Pamela Sargent lives in Albany, New York. Her website is at pamelasargent.com.

Made in United States
Troutdale, OR
08/13/2024

21959102R00065